BOOKS BY ROBERT WATSON

POEMS

Selected Poems   *1974*
Christmas in Las Vegas   *1971*
Advantages of Dark   *1966*
A Paper Horse   *1962*

NOVEL

Three Sides of the Mirror   *1966*

SELECTED POEMS
ROBERT WATSON

ROBERT WATSON, 1925-

SELECTED
POEMS

NEW YORK ATHENEUM 1974

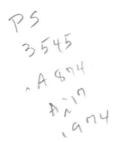

Poems from the following previously published books are included in
this volume:
A PAPER HORSE: copyright © 1960, 1961, 1962 by Robert Watson
ADVANTAGES OF DARK: copyright © 1963, 1964, 1965, 1966
    by Robert Watson
CHRISTMAS IN LAS VEGAS: copyright © 1966, 1967, 1968, 1969, 1970,
    1971 by Robert Watson

Library of Congress catalog card number 73–93706
ISBN 0–689–10602–5
Published simultaneously in Canada by McClelland & Stewart Ltd
Manufactured by Halliday Lithograph Corporation,
Hanover and Plympton, Massachusetts
Designed by Harry Ford
First Edition

NOTE

These poems are not arranged chronologically in order of composition or publication. They are evoked in clusters. Historical time to me is an illusion. I can never remember how old I am or what happened in what year, so I hold to simultaneity rather than continuity. Clock and calendar time exist, I guess, and I know when I look in the mirror; yet Chaucer and Homer, to me, seem young contemporaries while Milton and Wordsworth seem like elderly gentlemen. What appears out of time is the elegant; what is ordinary is the grand. A naked man and a naked woman in a sunlit garden present culture in its highest form. A garden is not a wilderness, anymore than a poem is. History must not be neglected, yet should not be thought of as linear. Stars and snowflakes are great stabilizers for lovers, as are flowers in vases. So lyric poetry is one of the better defenses against the barbarities of war and politicians, a counter rhythm to sequential time. We all live and die in ways teachers, governors, clergy, press and philosophers rarely recognize, tone deaf to rhythm. To govern is to misunderstand, to follow is to be diminished. Considering particular lives, though, what else can most individuals do? Gamble? A dice game, two lovers, a city, a small child: each has, as the seasons, the planets, its own rhythm, in time, out of time. And so these poems have varied rhythms—and varied forms or shapes, hopefully not imposed but arising out of the nature of the subject and of language.

CONTENTS

I

II

* *Poems hitherto unpublished in book form.*

III

IV

V

VIII

IX

LIGHT VERSE

I

THE RADIO ASTRONOMER

A radio astronomer in Utah lifts his ears
Over the moon and stars, sets them at empty space.
It's 3 a.m., a quiet hour. Beneath the moon it snows.

He sets his tape recorder to the ears, takes a coffee break,
Looks out the door at unintelligible random snow,
Its soft sound, drifting, each flake gorgeous as a number

In flight, gorgeous as stars and planets, their slow sounds
From long ago, cries amplified of stars in flight,
Sounds of the dead, the untranslatable tongues

Of the universe, where life other than this may be
Or was, surely, somewhere among the galaxies a signal
Could he hear it, in some recess a sound of familiar life.

Again he listens: the sounds seem random, or does he hear
A wheel turning, the click of dice, noise of cards dealt out?
A casino in the heavens? The powers wagering there?

He listens, tries to tie furniture of our lives
To each separate sound, sound to sight. The dice fall again.
The roulette wheel spins, slows, stops on an invisible number.

These sounds bring no grand music, no vision that Milton
Or Michelangelo knew. He unwraps a sandwich,
Pours more coffee. The sounds, he thinks, are random:

This is a universe of luck and chance. Galaxies
Spin in flight like snow, rattle in space, are gone.
For a while light lives, sound lives

Spinning through valleys and mountains of empty space:
God in sound, the great gambler sending in flight
The dice, the stars, the snow at 4 a.m. in Utah.

At 5 a.m. home through snow in bed he touches the breast
Of a galaxy, hears the dance of the heart and the lungs,
Feels the cells gather and shower, his children waking.

The sun explodes in the bedroom. The universe
Is gone: He falls to a soundless sleep, a corpse.

4

It's down the black hole for all of us,
The largest stars, Alice. Take Swan X One,
An invisible obstruction to our view.
Once a star, burnt out, it squeezed
Itself to a ball, so small, it turned
Inside out like a glove into a black hole,
A throat that swallows all into an eternity
Where time is space, and space is time.
Confusing? You bet. I think of other
Black holes: a grave, a vagina.
Age and gravity cause us all to shrink
(A hard-on is a great comfort in life
At my age.) Robert Hjellming says maybe
All matter goes down black holes and arises
Through white holes to another universe.
Maybe not. Why do I think about
Swan X One? Why not cats
Or flowers, simple mysteries in my own yard:
A gopher hole, the gopher itself? Because
Swan X One can neither be seen nor heard,
Because paddling it treads water, because
Swallowing it reduces all to
The immortal.

PLANET EIGHT

We clambered down in airtight suits to the ground
Of Planet Eight where the temperature
For us was cold. The sky was green and windless,
Our feet sank into dust that felt like fur.

We marched toward mounds and tall stones we thought
Must be a town, marched through a plain of dust
Where nothing grew, no tracks of bird or beast.
Under the layer of dust was a crust

Of rock. Our mallets tapped the house-high mounds.
We bored holes. Our gloves rubbed dust from walls of stone.
We found no sign of doors, no carved words.
A light flashed from our capsule, then our phone

Clicked with orders to return. That was all
I saw on Planet Eight, that stillbirth
Or corpse: we would have welcomed rats or flies.
But on the long weightless flight back to earth

With my life's high point shrinking to star size,
I dwell on the dust, the stone mounds, a life
Without life. I land on our stranger planet:
I look out with hostile eyes.

LUXURY FLIGHT FROM NEW YORK TO LOS ANGELES

After hot towels, the Girls serve caviar.
The Captain says, "We are thirty-five thousand
Feet over Lake Erie flying 600 miles an hour."

I see clouds like icebergs; the Girls serve "fruit de mer"
With wine. The Captain says, "It's 58 below outside."
My headset plays Brahms; the Girls serve orange liqueur.

Over Iowa they turn on the movie. "It's fair
Tonight at Los Angeles," the Captain says.
"Now we begin our descent." And I am here

On a red rug. I move by a conveyer
Into a canyon of automobile light
To my new life, my heated pool, my cooled air,

My white walled house with orange trees and stare
From my bedroom window at the blue lighted waters
Of my pool, all as if I had died and am buried here.

Twing.   Twing.   Twing.
                                   Splash!
An arc of flesh passes, has passed,
A head rises: over so fast.
Such grace, when others dive.

But I upon the plank tremble
A lifetime there. The pool,
Ten miles down, is dry concrete.
The upturned mouths, if I could hear,
Say "Die!" The next comes paddling
Up the rungs. "Die!"
                    Twing.   Twing.

I fling myself, my arms wings,
Then stretched, all stretched to needle
Sharpness. Nothing. Nothing . . .
Splash.

     My head rises
From my grave, from my bride.
I dry myself cocksure.
                    Twing.
Above me. My foot on the first rung,
In fear again my heart says
                    "Die . . . Die."

Flood from the first flash
  Earth swims around the sun in you.

The Sun swims in you too,
  Circles with its planets
    The center of the Milky Way.

The Milky Way swims in you
  Circling the Virgo Cluster
    With its thousand galaxies.

Sea of Light
  Where are we going?
    Where am I going?

I lie shirtless on the beach,
  My head spins,
    I swim in Massachusetts Bay.

I am swimming in water
  In the Sea of Light.
    Where am I going?

The day spins off to night.
  I see the Milky Way.
    Where is it going?

I am going to sleep
  In the circling bodies
    In the Sea of Light.

II

Mornings in Mantoloking in sunny August are best
Immortal sea dotted with sails of white, white hulls,
white foam
Umbrellas, yellow, green, blue, a garden in eternal sand
Where gull and piper stand.

The houses of Mantoloking float on the sea
Great wooden arks with turret and filigree
Summer homes of the late nineteenth century rich
Whose architects dreamt of castles, shingle, porch
And glider. My grandmother, a young lady with parasol

(I imagine)
Strolls on the porch, her eyes on a white sail.
My grandmother died last year
At 94, and the houses of Mantoloking all sank
In the night in the sea.

Was I moving through the invisible glass
   Between life and death,
When I walked through the glass door
   I thought was open?
The glass fell on me like icicles or knives,
   My clothes turned red and then my eyes.

After the nurse sponged my face the surgeon
   With needle and thread
Mended me as if I were a tattered coat.
   "You will be the same as ever
After a month on crutches and two with a cane."
   But I am not the same.

I would have sworn our sliding glass door was open,
   Nothing between in and out.
In daylight I walk as a man in darkness
   Hands out to feel
What the darkness holds, to test for walls
   That shatter,

For invisible curtains between what we see
   And what we think we see
On rainy nights staring beyond the windshield
   Or out the kitchen window
Washing glasses in the sink. Telescopes are useless.
   Everything we cannot see is here.

Drowned in my dresser under a surface of ties,
The photograph of you your aunt sent stiffens.
I stir, with half my life or less to come,
The watery figure of a lover now a nun,
Who half my life ago swam arm in arm
Under a lake unseen with me. Airs end.
I choose orange from India, knot the silk.

Even the clocks are not like ours
The numbers, if that is what they are,
Are different. I guess it is a clock.
(They refer to it as if it were.)
I don't understand one word of their speech
Or writing. I couldn't name one dish I ate.
Of the drinks, only water was familiar.
The old man his wife and I
Were fatigued with talking in gestures.
The years, the years! Next day again
I admired the fabric of their quaint clothes
And on our walks the old man would point
And name trees and flowers I had not known . . .
But I had—really forgotten—had known once.
It was as if I were senile, not the old couple.
I—maybe the three of us—were disturbed.
I asked myself will my children voyage out
And return to me as aliens, as if from
Another age, another planet. I blessed
My dear parents, and beat my way home.
To a wife who looked older, to children
                                    Who had grown.

In my embrace
At night a tree
Took on a face:

Limbs pressed back
Lips sprang
From the bark

Then the pine
Turned its boughs
Again to pine.

I am part tree now,
As seated on stone
Part bone, part stone.

on Halloween
(How near the dead the children seem)
Past skeletons, witches, and ghosts,
All children among the night-lit orange
Of pumpkins, leaves, my cycle coasts.

Shall I frighten the dead back to bed?
A roar. One more scorching up the road
And done. Dead leaves, the dead, like blood
On my hair, a crown my stiff fingers
By our porch's pumpkin-light I shed.

I pull blinds, blow out our pumpkin.
Our unmasked, exhausted children sleep.
Then down the chimney, or my mind,
Close-mouthed ghosts float in procession.
Around the living room they bend,
And near the end I think I see
Both our children, my wife and me.
A sip of cider clears my head
Of all nonsense about the dead.

I need not cycle to arouse
Or drive back the dead who nurse
Me with cider pressed of the fruit
From our apple tree's now bare arm
Burning in the fireplace. Up, out
The chimney sparks fly like stars. Warm
Stars fade with sparks. I float to sleep.

Is nothing private in our house,
Nor in the grave, nor universe?

I drop last year in the trash basket.
I open the package holding the leaves of the new,
My thumb slips, and the new year leaps in the air,
The 365 days explode, hover,
And lie dead on the floor.
The floor is heaped with days yet to come.
Shall I pick them up,
Order them by months, the days of each month?
Would it be worthwhile to re-make
The neat pile of days and weeks?
I stare in the trash at last year.
Is there a day I would like to retrieve,
Spend over again? I can't think of one.
I close my office door, leaving the new year
In its random disorder for the janitor
To pick up, drop in the trash along with the last.

A VALENTINE FOR A DRUGSTORE CLERK

I come for pills to cure me of
Some pain in my head, in my chest,
My heart. I see you and forget.

"*Lucky Strikes,*" I say.

I don't know you, you don't know me;
You know I smoke, I know you make change:
You drug me with your lanky form,
Your long fingers ring up the price,
Your blonde braided hair, a crown, and all
Your entrances and exits are rung
With bugles, fife, and kettledrum.

You hand me cigarettes, my change,
Which is your change unknown to you:
The notes of your voice are the notes
Of a flute, your fingers the wings
Of birds. The drugstore lifts with light
From your eyes.
                    "Here is your change."
"Thank you."
                    I strike a match, light up.
I forget my pills, all is well.

Both on their way to bed
Meet in near collision:
The hearse with forty cars of mourners never stops
And stalls the bride and bridal party
At the intersection.

At church a florist shifts flowers in a hurry;
The groom arriving much too early
Finds room at last to park.

After their nuptial flurry,
The couple worry in the dark,
Think the hearse slips back
And dumps its freight between them on the bed,
A corpse who reaches to the bed-side table,
Pours down their last champagne,
Then snores,
And in the morning gone—so goes their story.

And here goes ours:
The day after our marriage,
Not knowing how to sail,
And only told to watch the boom,
We ran an iceboat at ninety down a lake
And struck another iceboat
Bearing another bride and groom;
Both boats fell to kindling
But were we given any warning?
Well,
Our car was rented from an undertaker,

And didn't the flowers at the altar
Have a very pungent smell?

Over us in bed together kissing,
The night rides,
Dumps a splintered ice-boat, its shrouds,
The universe in our bed, our children's beds.
The arteries of heaven run bursting with cars.
"There are billions of galaxies," I read,
"And a galaxy contains countless billions of stars."

He comes in my daydreams
Asleep on the kitchen floor
His head on pillows
Body like a cat's curled
Breathing the sweet oven gas.
"Half in love with easeful death,"
He quoted Keats. He was twenty-two.

A quarter of a century has slid past
I soar now toward fifty alive
And drink my morning's coffee
Near the sun drenched stove.
At times these daydreams turn around:
I am young pillowed on the kitchen floor;
He is aging, fretful as he drives to work.

TO DRAGONS IN HIS CLASSROOM

I cannot fret about those who yawn dreaming
Over books that speak to them no more than grass
They watch outside our classroom window.
Let them dream: their dreams are books enough.

Nor will I fret about those with troubled eyes
Searching through deep foliage of words
For the lost palace they may never reach.

You! I fret about *you* who see
The still pool in the palace garden,
And declare without equivocation
That it is not there,
Or being there it does not matter.
You fret us while we feed you:
Your mind clicks out answers like an IBM
Into some trash can of your brain.

Now if a star spoke to you, on hearing its star talk,
You could repeat its message word for word,
Then swear the star had not spoken, not one word.
And were you rich, as surely you will be rich,
And if a precious book, a diamond or a star
Were up for sale, you'd buy it.
You could tell better than I what each said,
And then deny that any spoke.
When everything talks and nothing speaks to us
We move away. You move out,
And by some calculating clicks become a grand dragon

Lodged on treasure,
Some great legendary cold fish for us to gag upon.
Certainly you never seem to gag on us.

I fret about you who will never be numbered
Among the dead to whom we come and who come to us.
Can the dead breathe syllables of life
Into the machinery of your mind?
Will a blade of grass speak to you?
And will you answer, "It spoke a green word."?
Your speech will make that blade green,
Give it greenness as it has given you a word.
With a word you can call up the dead,
Give them life as they will give you your life,
The youth you lost.
Then you may wander searching through deep foliage of words,
For the lost palace at the end
Of the story that you read,
To the pool where, reflected at night, you will see
A prince kissing the rescued princess,
A star, the grass: yourself.

Yet if this prophecy does not come to pass,
If when you throw off your iron scales,
You are instantly burned to a cinder

By another dragon's breath,
Then curse me at your death as I curse you now
Coiled on all that treasure:
You—as books, stars, and grass—speak too,
Teach us a word. You teach us "Dragon,"
That dragons are real.

I shiver for you who sleep
Deep below the snow robed ground
In soundless cells, whose needs
Are none, nothing more must be
Sought by you or brought to you
Immune to common cares of us
Who want the brief green of spring
Or love. In death's row we wait
Breath's end to go to your sleep.
My sleep now brief in my warm room.

CONVERSATION AT LUNCH

I DON'T KNOW WHERE TO LIVE, says Donald Hall.

(I have made darkness my secret place; clouds
And waters my pavilion where I look
Over my city, my forests, up at stars
Unlighted. I rub two sticks, like two words,
Rub the unawakened woman at my side,
I rub two sticks.

             At the public table
I rub a match against a matchbox.
I light a cigarette. I blow smoke. I look
Down at my breast pocket far as England,
Where he goes next year:
My secret place under my pocket clicks,
A dance of sticks while my mouth, old gossip,
Spills the beans as if beans were rain,
Thunder, lightning, the world in flames. I cough,
Drop the world in the ash tray, light another.

                In my breast pocket
With matches I touch my child's skate key
And rub it like a rabbit's foot for luck.)

I DON'T KNOW WHERE TO LIVE, says Donald Hall.

(I am lunching in a public dining room,
A brown pavilion joining common men.
The new waiter so slow to bring our steaks
Is me. It takes the rubbing, the joining of two words

To make humanity: one is "know,"
The other "live"; but "where,"
The frightened sentinel on the wall,
Parades between
Rubbing his gun as if it were a woman's thigh.)

I DON'T KNOW WHERE TO LIVE, says Donald Hall.

(And other than here) NEITHER DO I.
(I have made darkness my secret place
And I rub two sticks to start a fire.)

YEARS AFTER THE DEATH OF FRANCES GLUCK

I lie at night on a warm summer's grave
In Provincetown, a practice death.

A bell rings:
"Luck, good luck," it sings your name.
Why should I get up?

You wore a little silver bell around your neck
And ran at me and stooped
And rang your bell and mooed
Like a cow.

Tossed by a motorcycle
Your head did not ring on the pavement.
And no "moos" from your coffin could be heard.

In the graveyard on the first welcoming arm
Of the new world far from your burial plot
In North Carolina I hear you yell to me,
"Let's ride in that new car of yours

And smash it all to hell."
What a swift arc from seat to curb.
"Love" was your most popular verb.
I'll place a sign around my neck
For you, reading
PLEASE DO NOT DISTURB.

I look in the harbor water.
　Behind my face
I find the usual debris:
　A hermit crab,
A rusty can, a bottle, and then
　The shadow
Of a ship turns back the water
　To water
Until water is all I see.

The lives I've almost lost are eight;
I've lived by luck and luck alone.
I've seen three wars smoke up the sky.
Why does a fat, grumbly woman
I have not seen for thirty years
Sigh to me on moonlit summer nights?
I smell her marigolds and taste
Fresh strawberry on my lips.
Is she my muse? That ugly tub
Who never spoke a pleasant word.

Walking to Sadie's in moonlight
Round the lake's rim, down the mountain
To her cottage, an ice-cream store . . .
She dipped the largest cones in Jersey.
Three hundred pounds of gloom. Back up
The mountain by the stream we children
Ate climbing to our dreams. And now
I have children taller than I.

Was she Aphrodite in disguise?
My wife says, "Watch your weight!" Woe's me.
I sigh and grumble over beer.

I kissed my first girl walking home
From Sadie's, lips licking strawberry,
Our feet wound in the mountain stream.
Next day Hitler marched on Poland,
I caught ten speckled trout.
The future drops its noose around my neck.
A car pulls up: my children home
Safe from the Dairy Queen. Hurrah.

No one is worthy, few are sane;
It is seldom that everything
Is as right as rain,

The rain that falls on me and you,
And all the flowers and all the tombs
That mark the dead of Truro.

Everything yesterday was as right as rain,
My arms were strong, our children young,
You were good and I was sane.

Now the rain has turned to sleet
Our eyes and ears are clogged
With cold, our hearts beat

In fear of judgement or of rot
While we select our burial plot.

III

SO, SO

Do numbers torment him? I at least bleed.
He never says. I never say . . . beyond
"How are you, dear?" "Oh, so, so, so—so."
Bees never sting him mowing. I get stung.
I move my hands among kitchen knives, needles,
My trowel, the thorns of my roses, cats claws.
The cat purrs on his lap, never on mine.
"What's new today at the office?" "Nothing, nothing."
Our children live in envelopes that come each month:
They might as well live in graves for all
We know them now. For thirty years I've loved
Him. And he me. Or I wouldn't be here. Or he
Wouldn't be here. Apple of my eye, the smoke
Rises from his pipe. The newspaper waltzes
In his lap. My knitting needles go clickety, click.

I live among sharp points and cutting edges.
And he an actuary for Prudential Life
Lives in probabilities. Does he dream in numbers?
At least my needle pricking draws blood.
I know what hurts me. He sighs in the abstract,
Abstracted. I love him. I love him.
Just to hear him breathe or cough. I love him.
"How are you dear?" "So, so." I'll lock the door.
It's time for bed.

I swallow my orange juice, I chew my toast.
I pray, I pray for a usual day
That moves routinely from stop to stop.
I read of a wreck on the IRT.
The elevator stops on the 30th floor.
Am I afraid of life or death or wrong?
If wrong it is? I dictate, "Gentlemen:
In the matter of . . . " Done. All is well, yet
I hear her typewriter play *liebestod*.
So reckless in dreams, compounded at six per cent.
Is *LIFE* what others have? I have heartburn.

For eight years, eight hours a day, yet not touch,
Not say. And said and touched what then; what then?
My wife smiles up from the blotter. Noon time,
The straight and narrow I have followed narrows
To buttermilk, my cream cheese sandwich,
My untasted jello. If I ask her
(Her glasses flashing in the haze of noon
Her hair gone from brown to grey), will she say,
Her vocal chords sweet as cello strings bowed,
"Oh love requited is love lost?" But still, still . . .
The stars are separate and the trees. What luck:
She here . . . at home a faithful wife and cat,
At home her needles go clickety-clack,
Here the keys go tat-ta-tat-tat.

In this sheltered world of home and office,
Office and home where lust and rage are banned
I lust and rage in wilds of sleep. Blessed
Are my days, this rich unvaried life.

The children are well, the weather
Cool for Los Angeles . . . What can I say?
If they are content, how can I be content?
A three day visit is all I can bear.
After praising her roses, her fudge,
The Christmas hand-knit sweater I can't think
Of more to say. Their yawning, endless, wordless
Nights inside. He rattles his paper, her needles click,
The cat purrs. How did their marriage stick?
I shed that boring prick, my husband
Of four years without a qualm. Do they live
In dreams? Dreams of what? Have they had
As I did and do, lovers? Those rabbits
Gave birth to a tigress. Mother, Father,
You move without moving toward zero.
Your last years. So I say *orange trees*
Are still in bloom. The freeways are. . . .
Highways at home, freeways out here.
In Los Angeles we've chucked over the old ways.
Why else would I be here in the land of tomorrow?
I live in Shangri La Complex with pools, palms.
A movie make-up artist, I move with sound-mixers,
Splicers, set-finders, starlets, stars. The door bell!
What will it be? A porno prince? A surfer king?

Lights off. The struggle to find sleep.
My cat's sleep comforts me. I touch the wall.
The wall is an extension of my arm.
My neighbors will keep me from any harm.
It's not thieves I fear. It's . . . I don't know.
In the apartment next to mine a couple live
Whom I only know to say "hello."
Upon the wall, their bedroom wall, I touch . . .
I wish, I wish some flow of warmth
Would circle back. The radio is human though:
Its little light and sound dispel the gloom
Until at times my mind finds in my bedroom
Memories of gaiety, I read, that others have.
The little light outlines my bamboo plant
Upon the bookcase full of mysteries. (My turtle died.)
I don't like birds. My pay check arrives
Each month, and keeps me, a kept woman.
O were I! The memories I'd have to tick
Me off to sleep. The frozen orange juice impatient
For my lips. The coffee seething. The sidewalk,
Agonizing for my tread. The world awaits my rising
And as I've always said, "Let the world wait."
As it has always treated me, I'll treat it:
Like so much dirt. Some day soon I'll meet
My Maker. I wonder what my Maker's like. I've always
Pondered that since he made me. I press the wall
At the side of the bed. The radio hums . . . It's . . .
                              I don't know.
If I warm some milk the cat will think
The milk's for her. Bamboo. Bamboo.
Now that's a word to put a mind to rest,
To rest before tomorrow brings office
And endless rat-it-tat-tat. Bamboo.

I have a cold; my girl, my boy have mumps.
John takes books nights as drugs to sleep and sleeps.
In the bathroom under an eight-watt night-light,
I test my breast for lumps. As in High School
When we studied Latin in the dark, I am
Still almost beautiful. George, I am forty;
You are seventeen. Bandaged in night-light,
My hair tinted the amber of iodine,
I spend a private hour in the mirror.
My glasses off, radio turned down low,
You are forty, George; I am seventeen.
Hell, there's that tub ring of John's, John didn't clean.

DIVORCÉE

I have rolled my shopping cart
  Down a million miles of aisles
Without a single accident
  Where I could say, "I'm sorry."
Or hear I'm sorry said.

I had my hair dyed red
  And spun tassles from my breasts
In a tavern filled with men
  Who gave me jokes instead . . .
Or twenty dollars to go to bed.

Instead of . . . They are all hard
  In stores, in church, in bars.
They want to touch, be touched
  But not touch me in my secret place
No flesh can ever reach.

I am spread out on the beach,
  The sun burns under my skin,
It lights the fuel I am.
  My sunburn is a charm against the moon
Who works against me in my rented room.

TWO STRANGERS IN A MOTEL ROOM

H E

If I showed you my Matisse nude hung
In orange light shed from my oriental rugs,
My rare books, my Savile Row suits
You would begin to know the man I am,
The man I have unzipped and neatly spread
Upon the chair, the man that even now
You hear I cannot shed, that grows back
On me when I speak. And you, now you
From the orange light behind my eyes become
That Matisse nude. Stay as you were, *as you*;
And peel me back again.
Hold my flesh as a wand and with your flesh
Transform us until you and I are
Nobody in any motel room anywhere.

SHE

Let me be that Matisse nude in orange light
In your living room with your rare books,
You in your London-made suit. Carry me
With your voice from this room, from my room at home
With children's crayon scrawls across the walls,
A torn, toy-splattered once-green rug and me
In my last year's Sears Roebuck pattern dress.
Press my breasts, my thighs to canvas thinness,
Whisper in my ear so that I know the man
You were, tell me
I am lovely, make your embraces lift me
To your orange light: a memory
From my long drive home from Mother's grave,
Your long drive home from wherever you came.

I let him in my room, lock the door;
Then lock the door of the room inside my head,
Where he tinkers, puffing at the knob,
Stoops peering at me on the bed,
Peering for what he, what the world thinks I have hidden.
I must call the janitor for more weather-stripping:
The wind is puffing through the cracks,
And chills my bones outside the door.

Now I lay me down to replay movies in the head-room
Caught in snatches between times when I am paged
By that usher selling candy with the curls,
Who hustles on my errands in a limousine I tipped him,
When another lady
Seeking servants in the theater caught his eye.
O I play on film a lady of leisure,
Retired, tired of my lovers
Whom I cut like sausage links.
As a rich lady I have seen,
Done all there is to do,
Seen all the stars playing,
Replaying under the lid where I have something I must hide.

In my travelogue you see me kiss the Pope
In my black sheath mourning . . . but mourning what?
I seem to have lost connection
At the Ladies House of Correction.
But here at St. Peter's on our screen,
I light a Roman candle for a body that is dead.
O the candy butcher sent me pills
For the common female ills,

And kept me in good humor
When the doctor cored my "tumor."
So I light a Roman candle for a body that is dead.
I rocket in a lap dissolve to Spain
To catch the ears of the matador
The bull will gore and throw to me,
Then the candy butcher and I can celebrate,
Eat oysters incognito at the Ritz—
As rich as Rockefeller—
In a suite of all black marble
Where I have something in a trunk that I must hide.

Now the reel seems out of order,
Projects blackness on the screen.
In the jungle night I hear a puffing,
A tinkering with a camera or a fuse,
And I must hurry, run bury what I have hidden,
But where, but what?
A shot! Loud as the door that slams,
And all the puffing, the tinkering stops,
Sound runs off its tracks
And silence cracks from the ceiling,
Until I am buried, trapped in my movie
After my theater has failed.

Yet squinting at my sockets, pointing sockets
To the keyhole of the room outside my room,
I see diamond rings are counting money in my purse,
And now I see a powdered face, familiar curls and fists
That batter, battering the door of the room that is my room
Until the door springs in. Thank God.
Here's the candy butcher. Light on, night done.
I'll stop the blood and put the coffee on.

But now I remember what I have hidden in the room
That is my room.
I have a closet, inside a trunk, inside a jewel box locked
That has a secret drawer,
And in the drawer, wrapped in tissue is a heart-shaped locket.
In the locket, if I alone unlatch it,
Is a magic mirror where I can make myself appear.

The movies are grinding love upon the screen.
I think that I might scream.
I heard love long ago
Driveling from my radio.
Stared at by advertisements from a bus
Of chewing gum, a teeny tiny truss,
My wanderlust has lost its lust.
Here lies a lady under my subway car
Who leapt and stalled us all at 14th Street.
(I can see nothing but her stockinged feet)
At my side I hear the fat
Soprano of a passenger:

"Screwing, I said to him, what's that?
Why not? Who cares? Screwing don't touch me, I said,
And what do you know he wouldn't do it to me."

Christ, I need a day off.
Christ, I need a day off.
Christ, I need a day off.

The fire engines sing a funny song.

It was terrible, the swelling, the squeezing,
    All that pushing and shoving
On and on.
    And the strain, the breathing,
Not knowing when it would end.

The mind going cockeyed,
  All that pushing and shoving
On and on.
  The pulse skipping, pores opening,
It was terrible.

And tired as if we had been grave digging
  All night long, on and on.
Then the hammering, and teeth slashing
  In the black heat,
The endless tunnel.

It was terrible all that:
  They call it love:
That's what it was, on and on . . .

The fire engines sing a funny song.

I've lived by washing filth away,
Dishes, pots, pans for forty years.
I fill garbage cans with bones.
All I touch soiled, spoiled: the world.

Why should I buy false teeth? I had
No appetite for food; I drank instead.
I tried, I tried: I changed my job
A dozen times each year, each time
Back to sinks again. Between jobs
I washed, rinsed myself in gin
And beer until the smell was gone,
Until I could not see my hands
That wiped the filth away. Content?
Almost content. "A little love?"
The women laughed. My teeth, I guess.

I saw her playing hopscotch.
I said, "Come and see my sick child."
I was the sick child on the bed.
A naughty girl to go with strangers!
She screamed. You tell me now she's dead,
Will never smear lipstick on cups
That I must clean. Poor, pure child.
I could not see my hands that day,
Those days I broke a hundred plates.
I loved her and not meaning to,
I saved her from the worst fate: life.

Monster, you say I am, but she
By the Mass of Angels is free
Of this filthy world, by me.
Father, I've scoured the world for Thee.

The whores of Times Square troop to their stations.
In orange wigs and stiletto heels they march
Past porno shops, a topless bar, halt, parade rest
On 49th Street, a pimp at each flank.

It is warm. It is noon. It is June.
Muggers spy out barroom windows.
Hotel clerks await their quota of false names.
The onslaught begins. The first shot is fired.
Will love conquer all? They peel off one by one
In orange wigs and stiletto heels.
Nearby a thousand peep shows buzz and fade
With films of conquest, atrocities of flesh.
Of man and beast.

(Is it the failed who seek out the more failed
Than they? And pay for what? Loneliness
Cured for ten minutes, lust cured for a day.)

What a wonderful piece of work is man.

A WOMAN'S QUESTION

"Will anyone ever come to understand me?"

"The character of trees is odd:
In Winter when we cover limbs
The Maples stand bare in the snow;
In Summer when we bare our arms
Maples reverse their stand and dress.
Or listen!
Take wind whose nature is perverse
To us. Scientists are no more help
Than magicians. Listen! Pine, Maple
Argue with wind on modes of dress."

"Will no one ever come to understand me?"

"Joined so tightly that no wind seeps between us,
I look down at a stranger
As you look up at a stranger.
I have never understood one Fall leaf,
The wind, or why we caress.
Is it not enough for a stranger
That the Maple tree, that you and I exist?
That on this late Fall night the wind
Has stript the three of us
All in the same season?
That we flutter in darkness without reason?
That tomorrow the wind in intensity
And direction may or may not alter?
Is it not enough

That we simply are
And cannot feel the wind blowing?
Though we are unknown and unknowing
That we are for a moment touching?"

CHRISTMAS IN LAS VEGAS (*A Widower Speaks*)

I shake its arm, the dials spin,
My life in bells, oranges, lemons, bars turns.
I can't lose, I can't win.
The hours shuffle by metallically here
Where neither night nor day nor hours are
Where under the pink, blinking bulbs
Over the fields of green felt
No one is young, no one is old.
The breasts of chorus girls swell like boils.

I bought a girl with chips last night.
O Doll, the beauty parlor styled your hair in pewter,
With lotions and light they plated your body with brass
Ignoring two white circles of breast
And one white stripe of ass.
All night we whirred and clicked
Bells, oranges, lemons, cherries, bars.
Assembled for departure in your blue fox
Your look pretty as any juke box.

I am a machine facing a machine.
I insert a quarter, shake an arm.
My arm is a handle, my legs are steel.
The dials of my mind spin.
I can't lose, I can't win.
My throat chokes with coins,
I spew quarters from my mouth.

Alone unriveted in the bath
Under the steady neon
A beast hisses, shakes its furred head.
I look out the window with my wolf's eyes.
It is night. It is night.

I have been a beast, I have been a machine.
Rabbit's foot and four-leaf clover, for Christmas
Let me hit the jackpot: make me a man
Who can hold a woman in tenderness,
Bear memories of tenderness,
Make my life in winter midnight moonlight spin
Where I will lose and I will win.

IV

How negligent they appear in this north light, our light,
Falling liquidly with dust from those high transoms,
Spilling over her form, still as a bowl of fruit.

She rests naked, carelessly it seems, on her side,
A long loop of pearls drops down over one breast,
Repeating the loop. Her pedestal, a couch draped
With a dusty cloth, stands before a flower papered wall.

From his easel, he contemplates her; she does not notice him.
She thinks entirely of herself, and he entirely of her.

Cold air and light roll and flash over her form,
Pour around looping lines of flesh that waver
Below her dispirited eyes. Her right nipple stiffens,
Gathers itself against the tide. Elbow, shoulder, back
All ache, constrain to hold her form in stillness,
To hold her body in suspense against the crushing sea.
She lies aching and arched, negligent and beautiful
Before the trembling green of an imaginary garden
Under surging lights on a cloth of red and saffron.

Her eye catches a glint of pearl; she thinks, unthinkingly,
Of her own pearl skin—a Venus bedded on a fanning shell;
Again she must feel that she is beautiful, an object of art
And adoration, her fire our light. But in her vanity
Does this elemental woman dream that she is everything,
The model of the universe, these pearls the stars
Of her heaven? If she feels this in her unthinking
Self-concern, why does she look dispirited then,

Like some bead-telling nun in sleep? Does she in gazing
On her flesh think of approaching death? On viewing
Her pearl skin, that wedge of darkness at her thighs,
Does she despairingly sense the history of the womb,
Those ancient shapes winding and unwinding on its floor?
And looking on her breasts recall the fruit she ate
When man began . . .? No. How can one so carelessly composed,
Stretched out on that dusty coverlet of fading red,
Ponder such thoughts in this cold north light?
What she dispiritedly ponders, we cannot know.
Yet she is the secret model of our dreams who guides
All wanderers in sleep: arched in stillness,
Beautiful, negligent before moving light of day.

Sirens in the street ruffle the stillness in the room,
Embroiling molecules of air; yet neither hears.

He stands, idly it seems, a brush dangling from his hand.
The canvas at his easel is blank, flat, white space.
He contemplates her; she does not notice him.

He stands against light and noise thinking of her
As yesterday he thought of oranges in a bowl.
Mapper of half-known spheres, oranges and women,
He loves neither, but uses both to quench a double thirst,
To wet a double palate. To him the spheres of each
Are always new and changing, yet the same and still.
Our galaxies—like floating trees—drift, bloom, give birth
And die in an endless sea of space, and she on the couch
Floats drifting, changing among flowers of the sea.
Not all his art can seem to fix, to still her shifting form;
Not all her art can still her shifting form for him,
Or calm the running sea of air and light in which she moves.

In anger at disorder in the light, his hand tightens
On the brush, ready to assault the space, to fill,
To flood a canvas with the wildness of this turning room.
But then, perhaps, he calls to mind some day of serenity
When a woman naked on a couch, an orange in a bowl
Were shadowed and still, quietly geometrical,
And that he must have thought was long ago, before his time.
Yet now somehow she settles down before his eyes . . .
She drifts into the garden, her swelling breasts flatten
Among leaves and flowers. She becomes the papered wall . . .
To him warring air and light remain without the scene,
As if a glass door framing her were shut and he stood
Out in a storm gazing in upon her sleeping form;
And he can no longer separate looping lines of flesh
From looping of flowered paper, spread, or beads.

He holds a knife now, loosely it seems, in his hand.
With one swirling gesture, as a master skater on new ice,
He cuts in wood one long looping line, a few swift arcs,
And he is done. Yet his canvas remains blank, flat, white space.

She rises aching from her pose of negligence,
And covers breasts which in her standing seem to droop.
We see that she is neither beautiful nor young.
Without a glance at him or his work, now dressed she leaves.

The print is black, a few thin lines of white cut in black.
A figure of a woman sits, not lies, with one elbow
On her knee, a string of pearls orbited about her hand,
Flowers looping around her form. This place contains no light
Or shade, seems nowhere we have ever been. And she?
She is supported, indifferently, by nothing we can see:

A black flower arched on a flowered wall of black.
In one corner hangs a blossom, its lips open over her head.
Inside the blossom we see nothing but darkness. . . .
Unhuman woman, if woman at all, in a world not seen
Even in our dreams, yet a world that must be everywhere—
We will suspend you in our rooms and meditate
Upon your simple shape winding there among the flowers.

Old oranges in the bowl glow like coals, fade to shadow
And go out. Light from the transom windows, our north light,
No longer spills over bowl or couch. All light is out.
He has gone. Yet in black stillness the scent
Of turpentine and oil moves into the invisible stream of air,
Spreading out the transom windows, and rolls slowly
Toward the scent of onions frying on a floor below.

Flags fly from a white tower's top in a green sky.
The dark couple at its base do not embrace,
Look up or down. This is the nostalgia
Of the infinite,
Of the infinite set on the retina,
On the base of the brain when the rain wipes clean
The brain pan and the wind bangs the pan on its nail.

Throwing their clothes on an invisible chair
Two figures float up in lavender air:
A man and woman alone in a dream
That they float
Without touching where they cannot be seen;
That each is who no one can ever be
In lavender air that no one can see.

We can show you a painting of us floating there,
Dreaming forever in lavender air:
We have taken the clothes from the walnut chair;
We are awake and dressed and stand with you all
And laugh at ourselves
Afloat in the frame on the wall in the hall.

WHAT CAN BE SOFTER THAN STONE?

Fourteen maidens listen to the *Liebestod*.
Thirteen maidens' faces bowed in music turn to stone.
All faces in repose are stiff and sad.
The music stops and rising from the sea of song
Go the washed faces of thirteen maidens, pink and glad.

Now fourteen, thirteen are maidens now,
Listen to the *Liebestod* again.
They drank the potion on the sail-slack ship,
And twelve maidens' faces bowed in music turn to stone.

After the fourteen maidens one by one have gone
I listen to the *Liebestod* alone.

That one whose face did not turn to stone,
Of the fourteen maidens is a maiden still,
One whom music could not, but whose words can kill.

Here is a museum for the poor,
A plotless tedium of legs,
Backs, busts bared above squatting cars.
We seek the vile that will arouse.

In this museum for the poor
In imagination behind
Glass and steel, our swollen ardors
Sag under magnification
Of what is:
                    The dreamt desirable
Bearing what is above desire.

The expected vile is innocent,
Almost beautiful. The modest
Beauty of bodies shorn of such
Vehemence of clothes becomes
Tedious to watch
                         as to watch
Encircling scrub pines burst luminous
In shots of lightning, dry and mute.

A SECOND LOOK AT VERONESE'S
"MARS AND VENUS UNITED BY LOVE"

Cupid with a dainty lace of silk
Ties Mars and Venus shin to shin.
Venus, wearing nothing much but skin,
With right hand on her breast squirts milk.

Mars in golden suit and cape of pink
With left hand fusses in her crotch.
Veronese! What a silly botch.
How can you call these Gods? I think,

Old Master, your painting lewd.
Standing Venus does not watch
The seated dandy fumble at her crotch,
And he disdains to view her nude,

While Cupid looks at neither one.
Behind, a stone Satyr, no doubt you,
Self-satisfied ignores the two.
United? Nonsense. Each is alone.

Now I see. The scene *seems* frivolous,
But eyes of Venus, Mars, Cupid
Are inward, deeply serious.
He cannot mate; Venus knows it.

Not all her comic oyster flesh
Will arrest his erotic ride
To red and swelling fields of death.
Mars' grey horse saddled waits aside.

"Whose work is this?"
"No man's work," replied Drowne.
"This figure lies within that block of
oak, and it is my business to find it."
HAWTHORNE.

Anatomy is the only subject.
My father in this drawing has the nose,
The chin, the lobeless ears of Bourbon kings.
This is his cobbler's bench. He died of drink.
This silver flute he made to suit my voice.
I carved at fifteen the first undraped male
In the new world: it is father, the Dauphin,
In gypsum. I call it *Despair.*
How he feared the secret police of Talleyrand.
From France to England to Nova Scotia
To Boston. He knew the foot, this cobbler
king.

As cobbler, doctor, painter, sculptor,
I know the body, bones, muscles, all flesh.
I always fill the lecture hall. I know
The dreams, nightmares beneath the skull. I loved
Dissection yet art is over medicine.
Our form is not ideal but beautiful:
The Greeks got it all wrong. Take it as is
Is my motto. Job is my great hero: *is.*
My children's catechism is naming bones,
The bones with their light coats of flesh, the beast
Our minds forever battle: the contortion,
The final loss when body slain by sword
Or illness slays the mind. We all must fail,
Father.

And I looked at him with many
bitter thoughts as upon the son of
a king, wondering of his strange
fortune, who, knowing not his inheritance, was a gladiator having
no call but to shed blood at
another's will.

The Brahmins in Boston look down at me:
A cobbler's son, a king's grandson. The forms
I make of stone accurate to flesh, to dreams
Is not for them. They choose the Greeks
Where life is smoothed away. For them
Marble. For me granite, the hardest stone.
I have the lobeless ears of Bourbon kings.

Between dances you showed
Me masks you fired in clay.

I

Mouth open, lips turned down
His small eyes protrude, the skin
Is lined, a crackled landscape.

(A month after the party your father died
In Korea where you flew.)

I try to understand your words
You try to understand mine:
Some we do, some we don't.

II

Lips up, he smiles the smile
Perhaps of an old man hiding
His dying from his child.

(Six thousand miles from there
I have three masks at which I look.)

Beautiful child you danced
Until my old lungs ached.
"You drunk?" "I'm not drunk."

III

Mouth open in full circle
As a fish in the sea.
A scream? a gasp of awe?

(You return in my dreams, Saung,
In black, seated, you talk Korean.)

Beautiful child, beautiful woman
Return from the land of my ignorance
That I can see three masks in one:
Your face, Saung Sook Yun.

V

This Halloween I'll just stay put at home.
An old ghost, my grave grows on me: warm shrubs,
An oak, asters, my flesh their sap, their leaves,
And their dead leaves my food; my voice the owl,
Wind or what I choose. I am content,
Content as I was never home in life,
My restlessness, mind scattered, gone to seed.

It took some getting used to I'll tell you.
At first my wet best suit began to shrink
And I swelled up like biscuit dough until—
The bone, wood box split. And I was born again:
A child playing in dirt, his parents gone.
Worst was that stone men stuck on top of me—
To keep me in, remind me of my name—
Heavy as my memory of childhood,
Weighed down with that trash they teach in school,
But the oak kicked down, weeds ate up the stone.
Here it's mindlessness that counts. A fleshpot
I was and am. You should have seen me glow
In youth, this youth with neighbors' bones
Dancing, mingling in dark. But that's behind,
Behind me in my wild phosphorescence.
A ripe corpse now of two hundred halloweens,
I find this grave is good enough for me.

Gossip has it my wife has turned black cat.
Agnes was always bad luck, bad luck for me,
Licked clean in her black Sunday dress she wore
To church to purr, claws closed in her black muff.

She thought she'd be a spirit when she'd die.
A spirit? When I'm solid as a mudpie.
To be dead you can't be squeamish, must be
A part of what Agnes could never bear.

Some lovers hide near graves as I once did,
Impatient, wanting my hard earned change,
Straining an hour in my lap; find, weep
That all this buckling on another fails.
Here it is our nature, law: I am my neighbor.
I am worn thin with what men above call sin.
Even in my dust age lust blows me on
To lace with other flesh, birds, beasts,
Grass and men. In spring a child once came here
And ate a wild strawberry at my foot.
And ate a little part of his great, great
Grandfather's left big toe. Do you smell smoke?

In fall when boys play with matches in the leaves,
Piled as comforters for my snug winter's nap,
I turn nervous, fear fire spreading out of hand
In which I die again, not to be buried
In cool, moist ground, sweet darkness of earth's flesh,
In which I mix, change each day, spread my arms
Out to the living world which lives in me:
My nightmare is fire that burns me to the clinker
Men call soul, and I am tossed to heaven,
Hell—who cares?—some other birth far away
From ashes of my accustomed lover earth;
To sit with that creature who was my wife;
To burn forever in fire of her yellow eyes,
Raked by metal claws: a mouse that black Agnes
In her superiority would have had me be.

THE MOUNTAIN OWNER

I have a mountain to run, father's once.
All year, years, I corkscrew up and down
Its sides on foot, on skis from Inn below
To Hut above to tend to skiers, climbers
Who come to crack their bones on mountain bones,
God knows why. In June snow still on its head
For fools to ski, I'm busy backside
Bottom flushing caverns for lost tourists
I mostly find. With ice pick and hand saw
I cut a man out the glacier once,
So neatly he looked alive in his cake
Like a man in a greenhouse. When I tire
I curl on a rock tongue in a mouth up top,
And from the throat I hear its insides
Bubble like a kettle, but I don't mind:
When the wind outside turns back snow like fur,
Or skins a whole cheek of rock, I rest here,
Drink brandy, and scheme to rent the mountain
For tunnels, mine for gold until I'm rich
Enough to go where I yearn to, away,
To a place of flatness where I can start
For somewhere regular, go straight, arrive, and stay.

"The Judge is dead.
The Judge is dead.
Throw him out the window
And spit on his head."

Each week I deal out years of jail.
Each year discard a life or two.
Each day for lunch a salad bowl.
(He sliced her head off in a fit;
She'd hid his shoes to keep him home)
Two bourbons evenings, never more.
I bathe at nine, I bed at ten,
I play croquet, cards, fish for trout.
(Law allows twelve fish in season)
The crimes men do. I see them all.
By now a million years of jail.
Inside a house, a cell of chairs,
We plotted crime 'til father set
Clock, wound sun, stars: his sentence bed.
Over our house, our cell, our crime,
The Grandfather's clock turns his face
To us, chimes his sentence for lunch,
Bourbon, bed, childhood, discarded lives.

All rise, eyes on me in black robes.
I strike my gavel, over-rule,
Spin lawyers through my wickets, thickets.
And ORDER, ORDER in the court.
But could they see me in the bath
Where I stand, mirrored, wet on scales!
Justice weighs itself, a fat fish

Of sixty: *Two hundred and four.*
This can't be me. Did she look so
When my morning's criminal struck
Off her head? Fish are not human.
And criminals? And I? I am a lover . . .
Of cards, croquet, the clock, and order,
Order in the court. I yearn to be
What I am, in robes . . . my bathrobe.
I take comfort in numerals.

The clock ticks like a heart. My heart
Ticks like a clock. Ice in my glass
Of bourbon clicks like dice. I shake
My fortune, my head. Grandfather chimes.
It's ten. I lock doors, windows,
Shut opinions in a briefcase,
Wind up Grandfather for tomorrow's
Judgment day. All is in order.
My wife completes her crossword puzzle.
The clock ticks. Dark. And all is well.

Swimming in bed I hear a noise.
Did I leave the faucet running?
Under the clock I hear a humming,
A stream flowing, line going out.
A feathered lure sinks through the ceiling.
Someone is trolling. I am dreaming.
I hear the clock and know it's raining.
Stars swim through wickets on our lawn.

Above the Supreme Court meets,
The Chief Justice, who wears no shoes,
Is setting the sun in his eye.
He strikes a ball through the wicket,
Winds his nose with a cloth. A cold
Today? What struck is now stricken.
And listen! The clock, the judge, says,
"Twelve."
            "Twelve what?" I ask. "Twelve fish
In season?"
            "Just twelve!" Chimes the Judge
In his bathrobe and whacks the bench.
So it is. I roll in a ball.
The gavel strikes. My sentence dealt . . .
A million years and lives discarded.
It rains outside the house, the jail,
And order, order in the court.

I run. I duck behind a truck.
How the leaves I step on snap.
A pigeon paddles into the sky.
One pigeon in a cold blue sky.
Snap. I drop the jewel case. Run.

From a rolling car a man sticks
Something he holds in his hand. Snap.
I touch my shoulder. My hand is red.
And warm as the sky is cold and blue.
Kick. I kick a man. Snap. I stop.

Why didn't I wait for dark to steal?
The sky, the sky in the rings
So blue. Then the sidewalk people
Strung like fence slats to kick away.
My hand turns brown as a leaf.

Someone is stealing something from me.

There must be something more than this,
Having whatever I wished to have,
Kissing the woman I wish to kiss
In this dark weatherless room,
In this wide, placid pond of bed
Shored with books, papers, pills, cash;
Our children safely stored, both wed;
And I insured against all loss,
Catastrophe.
          Customarily
My doctor sends me bottled sleep;
Everything so right, I want wrong.
I can't worry about the bomb;
All my named fears now long gone,
I almost wish a war again,
Where I can crouch behind the lines,
Listen to crack of shells as then;
My feet blistered in frozen boots.
Gone the first sweet match, first drunk,
First unfaithfulness. The worst,
The best over, done. Every dream
Of swimming, I swam, but the one
Up that last black, blank sealed
Stream.
          Once on a tour of Rome
I saw Him swim from Chapel's roof,
Cracked, peeling; saw angels burst
Through wood, stone until I almost,
Almost. . . . No; friends, wife would grin.

Smothered in our seasonless air,
Anchored in this tepid pond,
In Eden, innocent, ignorant,
Sane,
        how can I complain?

GRANDFATHER AT THE PLAYGROUND
DURING THE SABBATH HOUR

A woman screamed, some scuffling in grass;
The policeman shoved an old bum down the path.
I don't know what happened there;
Perhaps the bum had some buttons missing,
Or committed an indignity to a tree.
I saw an attendant cut the arm off a shrub
For being a little wild.
Only children can go wild
Without being arrested.
Only the smallest children, of course.

I move my three-year old grandson away
To play on a small plot fenced in by logs.
Inside he finds more logs, all stripped of bark,
Arranged in odd shapes for him to climb,
Swing, or even hide inside. Some look like horses
To ride . . . houses, towers . . . together a little town.
The parents watch outside on benches in a ring.

My father wrote to me sometime before he died:
    "Caution, my son, caution,
        Save all letters, send none.
        And when you marry, marry one
        Not for mind or beauty,
        But for submission,
        The quick commission
        Of housewifely care.
        And remember when the bell tolls
        It tolls for cash."

A man who was always very emphatic,
He finally hung himself in his attic.

When time is money, life is locked
Inside an iron box inside an iron room.
(In his will he left everything to himself—
All diamonds in a pouch.)
He never ate his cake, it just got stale.
He was a good man, they said, he never went to prison
Or any other place; yet at the end he knew
He had to pull himself up somehow,
Get a new point of view.

Now I married a woman for beauty . . .
That's a lie. I did what he said:
I stuck under his thumb,
And changed money in a bank for forty years,
Until this year, and, by Jesus, never misplaced
A cent of the blessed money.
The old banks inside were made like churches.
The officers sat in the apse and steered. A guard
In the choir, if you looked up, held a machine gun.
Today banks look like parks or gardens.
Anyway they try to look holy,
Or if not holy at least innocent.
(They get most of their ideas from the Bible.)
I like innocence best myself;
That's why I bring my grandson to the park
Sundays to play on slides and swings.

I told him little boys were lucky
They didn't have to work.
He shook his head and said,
"I work with toys."
Time is what you're doing and now
I work benches and my mouth,
Soon I'll be a bench,
A marble one with my name on it.

The children swing from logs.
(From horse to wall and tower)
They do what they want to do.
My grandson sees a log;
And that log is worked: he works a horse,
And if he fall hard, this old God from a bench
Will fly to earth, and with healing lips
Sew up the wound. He does this for children,
Only the smallest children, of course.

I'd like to be buried here someday
Under this plot of logs.
I'll ask the Commissioner of Parks
What a child is to do, who wants to work graves,
As I was taught to do.
My family buried me at four,
The miracle is I wasn't buried before.
I'll ring up father in his vault,
Tell him there's a big boom
In the manufacture of a toy tomb—
(He invented baby life insurance.)
Tell him everyone is playing Dead.
Well, life is a made-up affair;

All the little children know this.
But I forgot, forgot what innocence was,
And always, always followed the rules.

My wife—who thinks that dirt
Is the root of all Evil, and Good
The absence of dirt—
Says I'm in my second childhood.
(How she knows, I don't know,
Unless the spots on my shirt
Give me away.)
So I'm riding backwards now,
Putting things in reverse,
Getting younger every day.
Those diamonds I've turned into gold,
And I'm turning the gold back to dirt,
Anyhow melting it down,
From that gold I've liquefied—
You see that little log town—
Well, I'm making a universe.
You understand I just call it a universe:
The wonderful part is
I don't really know what I'm making,
But after years of being obedient and mild,
At last I'm kicking loose and running wild.

My grandson swings from log to log,
From horse to wall to tower.

THE NIGHT FEAR

I

First they stroke gently with hugs and sweet kisses.
   It will not go away.
Then they squeeze and suck, pinch the tender flesh.
   It will not go away.
They strike each other and bite until blood runs.
   It will not go away.
They lie touching without movement back to back.

It swoops and hisses over the dark room like a bat
   Or pendulum hour after hour
Over and over their still and sleepless limbs.
   "What is it?" "What's wrong?"
They ask themselves all the winter nights long.

At orange juice the children are lively as skyrockets,
   The furnace whistles, the dishwasher hums.
The *Morning Sun* says, STOCKS UP, WARMING AND CLEAR,
   CRIME DECLINES, PEACE NEAR.
The day spins on like a Merry-go-round.

II

Undressed in bed, their light out,
   Like a bat or pendulum
Back it comes hissing through the room.

Yet all is usual: the clock nods on the mantel,
   A child coughs, a neighbor dog snarls.
In their bathroom a nightlight glows on the tiles
   And on the silvery medicine cabinet
With its useless ointments, drops, pills.

They plunge at each other, clinging, clinging.
   What is it? What is the matter?
Then the bed rises, they think, through the French doors,
   Soars up, up over the roof
Until below earth shrinks small as a ping-pong ball,
   And the milky way enfolds them
As if they float through an enormous Christmas tree,
   Invisible branches spangled with light.

Yet still back and forth like a bat or pendulum
   It hisses through the roofless empyrean,

Then as a toboggan the bedstead slides
   Down, down past the moon
Through the French doors back into their room.
   The clock nods, a dog barks,
The bathroom tile glows safely in the dark.

III

At night now, swooping over their forms, the fear
   Like a meteorite
Hisses over the room, over the house,
   Beyond earth's atmosphere
Back and forth, back and forth.
   No longer do they cling and bite
And ask "What is it?" "What is it?"
   They think, two in one bed in one room
Will always hear some unnamed noise,
   Some terror buzzing in their hearts or skies,
Some fear no love clasps can lock outside.

To sink in sleep each now pictures a skater,
   His face muffled, his long scarf ends streaming
And snapping in the crystal air,
   His heart racing, swooping and hissing
Over the frozen, star-pocked pond of night.

Smoke he blew curled above his wife,
A milky way in bed. Outside
Their window and a branch, the night
Curled too. A question mark. He thought,
"The universe is curls." Smoke gone,
His cigarette mashed out, his mind
Was punctuated with doubt. The shade
He pulled blanked out all curls, all questions
Of night. The universe is not,
Is nothing he knew. But in sleep
He dreamt of Noah's ark and waked.
The emptiness is full, he felt,
And felt that he was curling up,
A mindless question of the flesh.
He reached . . . surprised his wife was there.
From the silent nothing, a black
High silk empty hat, a rabbit
Jumped. And so beasts disembarked
Upon the shore. In morning light
All furniture of life swam back:
He tore a plum from the window tree,
And ate his heart, the quack.

I've buried Troy, I've conquered Rome
And Hollywood. My crown, my head
Roll in a trunk with other parts
I wear. This is the good Lord's beard
I wore the day I made Adam,
Adam's fig leaf when I was he,
My horns for Mephistopheles . . .
Hamlet, Vanya, Lear, and Faust
Lie here. I shut the coffin's lid.
Curtain down, clothes, lives removed
I search the program for my name
In vain. What was it? I don't know.
Another life, name so long ago.

Find the birthmark on my elbow,
Tell me the nurse's error,
Of a changeling. "You are, you are . . .
The eldest son, the only heir . . ."
Curtain before he tells my name.

No more of men, no more of gods,
The dreams of men, the dreams of gods.
No more of parts, of parts of parts
Made up by men who made up life.
I'll play spaces between stars,
Dust rising from dancer's feet.
The world sprouts from my trunk, my limbs.
My leaves, our stars whisper: "You have
No name."
             I am now satisfied.

VI

Three hugest dinosaurs do not outweigh
That one hundred foot long whale who will strain
The sea for krill, four tons a day. Svend Foyn,
A man, found how to blow its twenty pound brain
To rice and still its thousand pound heart
For its forty thousand pounds of oil. Soon
The blue whale fewer than the whooping crane
Will be, who is a useless bird. Of old,
Churchmen said the devil was like a whale.
Soon we can sail dry seas empty of all
Monstrosities, and man alone can strain
The little krill, all food, thought for his brain.
There's life some say in smallest grains of rice.
Man must eat; killing is not good, not evil.
After waters are plundered well as land,
I will think
Of Svend Foyn who destroyed the devil,
A one hundred and fifty ton, toothless blue whale.

"May we visit you, Miss Burckhardt, my dear?
Come from behind the blinds you peer through.
Telephone and doorbell ring and ring,
You have spent your lifetime in not answering.
Now callers you should not ignore are here."

"I will go on unanswering all each day.
Silence! While I add infernal taxes up—
Federal, state, city grasp and grasp
What I have spent my lifetime saving.
Wolves at my door, callers, away, away!"

"We have come for you, Miss Burckhardt, my dear,
Not money hidden as refuse, breeding,
You have spent ninety years concealing
Under your sink, bill upon bill upon bill.
Now callers you cannot ignore are here."

"Will telephone, doorbell, voices never cease?
All night the beech tree knocks at my window,
Wind at door, rain at roof, dust at floor;
I can scarcely total numbers anymore.
When will you give, O Lord, this servant peace?"

"We must have you, Miss Burckhardt, my dear.
Take from your dresser that old brown sock,
Where you keep your house and strong box keys,
Limp on your cane, unbolt the triple lock.
A thief? Behold, I stand at the door and knock."

The knocking and ringing and calling at last
Shook up her head like a dynamite blast.
She limped to her dresser, to her sock for her keys.
She unbolted her door, but saw nothing there,
Not caller, not thief, not tree, dust, nor air.

Everyone could tell they had given up,
Abandoned amenities of attire, diet, soap:
She lean, face mean with fear or pain;
He obese, socks unmated, belches at the magazine
In which he looks and does not turn a page.
She would cry off and on.
They are themselves, nothing else, too far gone
To soothe our minds with any likeness
To familiar bird, beast, or fish.

An outrage:

They strung a spell over the doctor's office.
These wretches made us invisible and well,
Pick pocketed our each groomed ill.
They were so cruelly themselves, foreign and other.
Untended, their children bang and rain
Up and down the corridor like a hurricane.
They ruled the waiting room, this crude, poor pair
And they had renounced all that to us is dear.

Here at the end of the line
The night's final train stops;
In the last car the dark drops.
Here at the end of night
A clock shrieks, the wife shoots flak,
The children detonate on my back.
And red morning (Where is that sock?)
And red morning streaks in ringing:
O sweet ambulance of dawn.
Here at the wall of my desk
I command the envelopes away:
Hup. Two, three, four,
Fire the directives out the door.
I scream at the waitress to bring my bill.
O sweet salad why doth thee lie so still?
Here at the edge of the track
The hearse stands to take me back.
Listen, the wheels do snap and rave
Until at the edge of the grave
Where dark is as sharp as a knife
I flop in the tomb of my wife.
Here at the opening gate
I board a windowless car.
With the hiss of a connubial snore
It moves as slow as a star.

He's somewhere out there. I stay here.
Who's more in jail I couldn't say
Nor could he. I used to be afraid
It was a woman. Fat from beer

What woman would want that tub now?
Those wasted years I worried over girls
Or gambling when he was . . . just out
Walking or watching TV in bars.

My neighbor's husband he stayed put
All night. And did they quarrel.
He had a temper he couldn't control.
Her checkbook balance was out four

Dollars so he got his shotgun
Off the rack. She dove out the door
And ran until she heard the bang.
With her not there to shoot he shot

Himself and by gum died. We all
Need some outlet, but I stay home.
Let him go tramp in rain and cold:
What he's looking for he'll never find.

Let the houses fall.
Let them flick down those that choose
To stand in the brash wind.
Help the wind blow the whole town down
To a rubbish heap.

Send the Mayor matches.
Let him light the pile.
Let them dance around the flames
Until the wind has twirled the town away.

Let us, backs to the light of the fire,
Read some book against wind,
Against fire,
Pranks.

Let us read a book
Old, awkward, tedious as we
To hold against the clever wind.

Let us read a story
Of a man, a woman,
Who built a house
That men and wind and fire conspired against.

A story of a man, a woman,
Who reading a book
Yawn
Into the straight, steady rain
Of sleep, a rain of a late autumn
Day with nothing to do
But watch the fire sleeping in the fireplace.

A hand of stone on top of a tipped tomb
That pointed up to heaven once now points
Straight at my father's slumber where he lies drunk
In wet grass in shade of an upright tomb.

My father's fingers point along the grass
At nothing—unless at a dove who died
Under a bush, its wings outstretched, head squashed,
With father's empty bottle lying beside.

Age or vandals with these slabs have played
In time a crazy kind of dominoes;
Yet no one comes to straighten up the rows
Of tipped or leaning stones where father sleeps.

* * *

When they stretch together in wet grass,
Each pointing toward the other, I see
That stone and dove and man's ends are the same—
What father knew too well would come to pass.

No middle for him: a beginning and end,
An unending ending of his waking life,
A shade drawn daily against the living world,
A walk in blindfold to a borderland,

Where this stateless man sees, or dreams he sees,
The soft, welcome shadow of his lover
Waiting, secret on the river's other bank,
Arms outstretched, beckoning him softly over.

And there he lies peering over the water,
Weeping, without a passport for his crossing,
Lies on the edge pretending he is dead,
Ears stopped to cries of wife and daughter.

* * *

Do all men stray to dark, beyond our cries,
Fiddle with death, and listen to music played
By instruments of their sober trades:
Lawyers drawing wills, the surgeons knives?

Did these vandals race to end of reason
To find life under this life, and dig hard?
Or did they in wild love turn up the yard
To show us nothing is here, nothing at all?

For my husband let me have the vandal
Who will outrage the other life and leap in this,
Who will topple tombs and outrun scandal—
Beat Death in dominoes before we kiss.

* * *

Dear dreaming, wasted Father, floating
Further each day from my hardening memory,
I will let you slumber here, let you lie
While I move further from you tenderly.
O my dear dying, drunken Father, go floating
Softly to her dark, winged kingdom waiting.

The girls twist the radio
Until it squawks,
Something to do, to do, to do, do, do.
BONG swings the fist of the clock.
The druggist winds up a toy panther;
The black beast climbs a wire tree.
Then one girl swings the druggist
In dance until girl two
Flips out his wide red tie for something to do.
They run out, shout, "Old lecher, old goat";
And his bought squirrel teeth smile back
Saying, "Not one drug works."
SNAP goes the front door lock.

Two girls kick at the streets,
Frown in windows
Until their feet hurt worse than their hearts.
To do, to do, to do, do, do.
In her own home in bed
Each peers into a black sheet, her heart.
The black sheet rises, and each trembling asks,
"Is there a black panther loose in the dark?"
No. The black sheet risen shows
A widow sipping tea
Watching boxes wrapped for grandchildren
Under the Christmas tree.
A red squirrel stares from the almond-laden sill.
Each sighs in sleep, "Is that widow me?"

But Night stays up pacing the drugstore floor,
Frowns at the book, the magazine rack.
"I've read you all," says Night.
"For something to do
I'll dial WEather on the phone:
Night here, send me rush
Slush, sleet, then snow, and hard, hard blow."

The sick elm in front of the drugstore,
Alone without a bird in a limb,
Gives up the ghost, throws himself
Headfirst through the glass,
Smashing drugs, radio, clock.
Night, alive by a miracle,
Packs the one unbroken toy,
A black panther, in his bag,
Jumps over the fountain, the elm,
Black hat pulled down tight
Against the spreading light,
Hums,
Something to do, to do, to do, do, do.

VII

All houses stand in pools of black.
A police car's blue roof-eye trails
Me down this Fall night of drifting
Leaves. I drift. I drift. It's wrong
To fall in love so many times,
So many times. The yellow leaves
This Fall more beautiful than last.

They curb me with a siren cry.
"Destination? Your license please!"
"Nowhere. I can't sleep." O the stars
Warm, luminous as. . . . It's wrong
With half-dressed trees so lovely now
As you and they were and all are.
The blue light spins away in leaves.

Why don't I root myself in bed;
A black tree in rows, unmoving,
Of black trees? It's wrong to fall in love
So many times, so many times.

ADVANTAGES OF DARK

The sun
     Through cold slabs of air
        Over a slice of field
Between prongs of leafless oaks
     Through the double-glassed windows
        Through thick oil-heated air
           The sun snaps at you
           Asleep on the bed
     On the tan rug
On the oak floor.
                    Light thrusts
                       At your body
                          Chalks flesh in parts
                    Snips shoulders
                       Neck
                          Unstitches hair from skull
                             Shears head from pillow
                          Cuts out eyes
                       Divides your lips
                    Splits you from me.
Night assembled us
     Drew my limbs to yours
        Molded us to the bed
Clamped bed to floor
     Floor to frozen ground
        Bedding the dead
           Holding the leafless oaks
        Night spread us with black
     Seeded with stars
To warm our bed.

                    Until scissors of light
                        Shears air from field
                        Oaks from windows
                    Cuts you from me
                    From the bed
                        Bed from floor
                                Dissects you to particulars
                                Thumbs toes knees eyes hair
                        Snips you from the unborn
                    The living and the dead.
Light holds
     More mystery than dark
          Light cuts
Like a child
     With blunt shears
          Cuts
                    From an old magazine
          The pictures
     From the pictures
Name by name.

All the morning sun's lowered ladders
Do not reach you wherever you sleep.
Beyond my unsteady hand and head
You keep to rungs of darkness in day.

The evening winds tumble you through dark
From street to bar, car to car, lips not mine.
I smoke too much. The molten heavens toss
In space that knows no night or day.

At dawn I rise, at dawn you sink to sleep
And keep the night about you like a hood.
I walk to work, whistle. Birds whistle back.
They plug me to a phone from nine to five.

Outside my office white air flashes with black winged
Birds. I would sing at coffee break, fling
You through spans of light a song of light.
One clear night a year when the full moon

Lights up a new snowfall we can meet
At twelve, reach through our coats and touch
With snow wet fingers each others hearts.
I hold to night. You hold to day. The stars

Lie on the snow, all ladders fall. I walk
From the light side of the bridge to dark.
You pass me to light. We become each other
For a moment, and then say goodby.

VICTORY

Moving furniture around my room
I can move stars, the streetlights and the dust
In rolls below our chairs. I can change weather
If I want.

Changing the order of books in shelves
Christ marries Helen, Alexander leans
On Mother Goose. I can change all history
If I wish.

Putting on clothes I have not worn before
I sit on a shifted chair turning my body
To something new. I can be President
When I choose.

Opening the door to watch the snow
I walk frozen ground, past frozen trees,
Around the block, around. I can circle the universe
When I will.

Indoors I light a fire to warm the air,
I can move the chimney across the room,
Or doom the furniture in the hearth
If I please.

But you, like a frozen tree in frozen ground,
I'll walk around, I'll walk around the block,
I'll shift all the furniture in my room.
I'll move you yet.

I

"I am a young girl in love leaning
Into my mirror, dreaming.
Do I hear a rattling
In the leaves of my Catalpa tree?"

"I am a young man in love courting
A girl rich as the sea.
Does she hear me rattling
The leaves of her Catalpa tree?"

II

"Am I some spool to be unwound,
Mere stitching fed to the machine?
A broom to sweep up this day
And then the next?
Loneliness that sweeps in from the sea
Still rattles the leaves of my Catalpa tree."

"Wanderers not finding Paradise
Return home, some only in dreams,
And the first home is changed
If standing at all.
Loneliness that launched me on the sea
Still rattles the leaves of her Catalpa tree."

III

"We sit at last together, dried old gourds.
We listen to a rattling
That does not seem to come from leaves.
And we have lost our hearing.
What? Did you speak?"

How beautiful they thought they were
Until over his shoulder, on the table
She saw the ripe yellow pear—
Quaked, hugged her breasts
And thrust him out the door in fear.
Poor woman, her life undone
From a misbegotten figure
Of human beauty on the scale with one ripe yellow pear.

This tasty disease of desire,
Lady, for you and your kind
Makes a man of my years
Askew in comportment,
My words jagged against earrings,
Chaffing to perfumed necks.
To talk weather or politics
Would be more seemly, less honest
When you have chosen to appear
In a green sheath with your arms bare.
Indeed you have selected the topic
Of our talk, the sum of you
Which does not exclude physique.

Love? I'd rather be condemned to Grand Opera,
Crammed in those little seats, that muck in my ears.
I'm too sensitive for love. The act of love
Repeats itself, repeats itself. And you?
Without my glasses are much like the last.
This bed scrambling of limbs is commonplace
As plates of breakfast eggs. Our flesh is comic.
Such odd handles, pouches, spouts, and pipes
That twitch, swell, or spurt. Like dish washing,
Done, then time to start again.
Dignity?
Animals have it over man.

Sight. Lost sight of. Sight again.
Blurs become faces. I see you
There across the street. I yell to you
Not someone else. You, yes, you. Rush.
We rush from sidewalks of talk
To your bed of touch to strip
Off color. The plot thickens.
Denouement. The end. The end of us.
Our eyes focused, but our hearts blurred.

You search the sheets for a contact lens.
Again we see each other through glass
And drink to passion that was not love.
Our sight gave us no lasting vision:
You an ordinary woman,
I an ordinary man.
"Love is blind," you twist an old saw.
Look out the window see day
Hold out to us raw hands, snap
Its steel teeth. The sky opens
At dawn . . . like what? A pale red rose?
A toothless mouth? Did our lenses show us
Too little or too much?

He *would* notice her.
First afar, in his eye like a speck of dust.
Then nearer planted in the doorway of his sight
Until she would be a custom to his eye.
Sudden absence next!
He'd puzzle if his front-yard tree ran off.
And return, return gliding in circles
In loose clothes like long plumes.
He would wonder what foreign bird this was.
He would raise his eyes like barrels of a gun,
And when his eyes were aimed, she would hover
Without a smile, or frown, would turn to him:
Her eyes open windows to a dim fire-lit room.
Then close; with lowered head she'd pad away.
She'd never have to listen to his talk:
His feet would tell her scuffling through the forest
To her porch. And quiet, quiet. Words his weapons
Would never do. He'd scatter shot into the night,
Open the door, reach under and stroke the heart;
Then he'd skin her by the fire, but she'd poke him in the pot.

The wind we pull into our lungs, my cat,
Is breath of penguins, a Tibetan Yak.

It's cold. See the clouds fly to Florida.
Your ear warms my ear. A chow coughs in China.

You think we touch alone in our love story:
Smoke soars with drum beats from New Guinea.

We taste the faint last breath of a soldier,
Far away, dead under our evening star,

His breath on our joining lips, down your throat,
Into winds of your breast and heart, and out.

Your ear to my chest, we listen to air—
In and out, in and out. And then your hair

Whirls up into a gusty milky way.
You frown. "You don't love me, do you?" you say.

What can I do? What choice do we have now
Or ever? Let's go in, it's starting to snow.

FLYING ON COFFEE

A last, last kiss
On our last morning
So like the first morning
On the green rug
We hug on that green meadow
Sprawling with books
In bright jackets singing.

I high in you, in mind
Look a book on stars
On India, Africa
The sun through a crack
In the white drapes
Burns in our glass of coffee
Small as a skate wheel bearing.

The sun is in the glass
We pass the milky way
The coffee is night
Through your thighs
Look in my pupils
I look in yours
We have gulped down the night.

Damn! You broke it
The last glass of us
You broke the spell
I hear the mailman
Go put your clothes on
Pick up the glass
And get your tail out the door.

The last morning
The last broken kiss
As on the first morning
The shattered words
Our fingers bleed
On the green wool rug
It was the mailman's fault

Sorry
I didn't mean
You to dress
Shelve the books
Open the white drapes
To the street gnat thick
With other lives passing, passing.

All my most, almost love
From moistness of below
To moistness of above
Your lips, your hair I give

All my most, almost love
Bare on the rug lowly
In love we are to grow
No more sweetly to go

No more lowly to go
Gone from my window
Almost all, my most stranger,
                I guess.
Both above and below.

It is full
The tide is high
We pull

The sheets up
We clasp
And drop

After love
To sleep.
The moon

Swings on
Alone as I
As you by

Sleep divide
From one to two.

VIII

THE CITY OF PASSAIC

A Prologue
Can you hear my voice over horns,
Babble of all world's tongues,
Ancestor's words hanging in air
Thick with burning oil, rubber,
Blood of slaughtered pigs and men
Filling my lungs with dead ones,
Yellow leaves of reckoning—Memory,
Old mad mother in your shawl,
Sewing in the factory at the railway
Trestle, your garments never done,
Bless on your rosary my seed
That at last our child may be born
To build this city never complete
Rotting like your old-world teeth,
The unfinished city, throne of the world,
Of time, the City of Passaic.
Bend to me old seamstress in your kerchief
By the railroad track
In the whistling six o'clock dark.
Lie on your back
In your perpetual black dress,
Lie in our inheritance, cinders
On the track. Teach me your tongue,
Scream it out
Until the train's one eye comes.
Bless my rape, bless our Paradise,
Our only world, last world, Passaic.
Remember old mother in your bleeding womb,
Scream your story in my ear.
Light. Light. A locomotive comes,
A rain of sparks:

Old woman, old mother,
Bring an architect burning
Out of the tender dark and pain.
Turning in sparks, in smoke
Your age falls,
Falls like your shawl.

II
And some said the King of Gods
On the roof of heaven behind a smokestack
Wrapped in smoke heard a mad
Old Hungarian sewing woman
Crying rape under a trestle
Near the railroad tracks, summoned
A train's one eye that He might see
Into his chosen City of Passaic,
His secret unfinished capital of the world.
And there was his Son heaving in filth
With an old woman, a Goddess in disguise.
Then the King of the Gods spoke,
Words rising as smoke, falling in sparks
Over the fornicators under the trestle
By the tracks, where the locomotive
Throwing sparks, brakes for its stop,
Where passengers from Passaic,
Lungs filled with burning oil,
Rubber, blood of slaughtered pigs,
And men, in littered cars snake
Down tracks to Hudson tubes,
And exhale Passaic in New York
In the air
In the world's red night air.

III

And some said the watchman,
His bottle empty on the roof
Behind the smokestack, descending
For more rye in Benny's bar
Across the street, descending saw
By the light of the six-o-five
A couple heaving in filth
In a shower of sparks and asked
The cop in Benny's bar,
Was a tart in the trestle set up shop.
And the cop said,
"He was no railroad Dick. Ha. Ha."
Til Benny brought his on the house,
And the watchman, one eye out the window
Should the factory burn down,
And one eye on Bella, the class sweetheart,
Telling jokes for drinks,
Keeping men in that old uproar
As when she led the cheers the day
That Benny kicked the winning point
And beat Garfield.
Bella, the class sweetheart gone to pot
Near the broad fields of Benny's gut.
Benny gives the cop his weekly cut.
At the Polish People's Home the watchman
Danced a polka with Bella once
Until his feet were hot.
"My God, the factory's caught a-fire."
With a gulp he killed his shot,
But halfway out the door
His shoe dropped off and Bella cracked,

"Spit in your shoe, in your shoe;
Use it for glue, use it for glue."
And one shoe off and one shoe on
He ran to find where *was* there an alarm.

IV

And I an old woman at six o'clock
Did not steal coal today at the railroad track,
After days of sewing, of thread and needle,
Loom or broom,
In a land whose tongue I am too old to learn,
A widow with two daughters,
Whose hope chests I must fill,
Have watched a young man watch me gathering coals
Beside the tracks, beside the mill.
Today I sent Stella to my sewing, for our coal.
Today I went to Doctor.
Today I went to Priest.
How my fingers they are stiff
How my fingers they are swole.

V

I am a girl in a kerchief
In Momma's old black coat.
All day I've done her work
At the factory by the tracks;
I did not speak to the workmen
Because Anna told me what men do.
Next year I go to a convent,
Or maybe a nurse in white.
I will not be like Momma,
And sew in a dirty factory

Beside the dirty tracks.
And I will not be like Anna
Who wants the boys to squeeze.
Last fast day I took no food,
Not even a slice of gum.
Down on my knees, I told my beads,
While Anna she smoked and drank a coke.
In bed to me the voice of Mary said,
"Stella,
You ate no food, you drank no water,
Stella, you are my blesséd daughter."
While Anna she smoked and drank a coke.
Now gathering coals by the track,
A white light comes, a flame.
I drop upon the ground, I shut my eyes,
I hear a thunder sound, a voice say,
"Bless our Paradise,
Our only world, last world."
And feel the arms of God squeeze,
And all the bells of heaven ring.

VI
I am Anna taking off my fur-collared coat.
I am as beautiful as the stars
In my movie book.
I take off my clothes in the mirror
And look at Anna, how soft I am.
The bells are ringing. I hear a siren sound.
A welcome for Anna come back to town.
They are burning the city down to the ground
For Anna, Anna, Queen of the screen.

VII

Over the horns, the bells of Passaic,
The four Wards of Paradise ring.
First at the Linden Hose,
Where black booted, coated, hatted,
Warriors of fire mount the truck
At the watchman's alarm.
The bells ring on the Rabbi's phone,
On the Chinese Laundry door.
The bells ring to the Star of Hope,
To Jehovah. Ring in the ears
Of Our Lady of Fatima,
Our Lady of Mount Carmel.
Saint Andrew, Saint Anthony,
Saint George and Saint John.
Saint Mary, Saint Michael, Saint Nicholas,
Saint Peter and Paul.
They ring in Russian, Polish, and Greek,
Byzantine, Spanish, in Slovak,
Ring over Moria, Zion and Padua,
Over the tracks of the Erie and Lackawana.
All world's bells ring,
All four drawbridges over the Passaic
Rise to the fireboat's blast.
All cars, buses, trains, carrying Passaic to the world stop.
All bells, tongues, clang over the flames,
Over the son, over the old mother,
Stella, Anna, Bella, Benny,
Over the watchman, over the cop,
Over the Beer Barrel Polka,
Playing in the juke box
In Benny's empty bar.

THE AFRICAN SHOP

*"My father went to war
In 1954
He pulled the trigger
And shot a nigger
In 1954."*

Behind wooden women, all belly, breast,
Hang zebra skins, shields, spears, masks for sale.
(Have they cookbooks where I can look up *Man*,
Some old dish new to me, a recipe
To make me strong as my long enemy?)
How silly I am! Still I pretend to buy
A jungle room, squat on the striped rug,
Chew, before fire, behind my mask, my shield,
A last sweet eye of foe. I tap a drum.
A black woman dances, all belly, breast.
Shrunken heads dangle on the wall. I laugh.
I tap the drumhead belly of my bride.
A foot taps back. Dark rooted in dark we sleep
Until the sun, a gong the salesman strikes
Wakes me. I steer my wife out, six months gone.

When we as old Africa, old China crack,
Go down, our room dismantled to a shop,
Will the buyer scan our cookbook for *Man*,
Some old dish new to him, a recipe
To make him strong as his long enemy?
Will I, my head shrunken in a photo,
See him in my steel helmet, strap on my gun,
Wipe from his mouth a small crumb of foe, see
On his rug, our flag, a white woman dance,

Nude as a movie star, shake out soft flesh—
All that his enemy did pursue—shake
To ancient music from our tape? Then,
Deep rooted in dark, dream in dream, they steer
Into the civilization of sleep,
Where armed the uneaten *foe* unmasks,
Fills the dark wall-less room. *He* is the dark.

Aristotle taught Alexander Homer's lines.
Alexander won his wars with *The Iliad*
At his side. Who rules?
A teacher, poet, a sword swinging king . . .
Or some woman whose dazzle clots their eyes?
A county of farmers won the known world.

MEMOIR OF A MINOR OFFICIAL FORMERLY AT THE AMERICAN CONSULATE IN ZURICH, 1946

Come from the far, dark distance back,
Sob on my shoulder, your blond hair
Spread like a fan over my arm.
Your Polish passport on the chair
Lies useless, our coffee is cold.
Consulate doors are now locked tight
Against you, caught at the border last night.

Come wrap your tired arms around me,
Sob broken German in my ear
Of family bombed, or boxed and stamped
"Siberia," and so I hear
The boxcars shunting in the dark:
At midnight your visa expired;
The *Fremdenpolizei* have marked you "Undesired."

I I

And what could I have done? I could not forge
A passport for every stateless one.
I let her go, blond hair fanning into snow,
Went on vacation with my countrymen.
From our chalet on the timberline we rode
Up frozen backs to a few black teeth
Hooked in the sky, then dropped down, far down,
Spraying white scales, to a toy town beneath,
Where we again started our slow ascent
Back up unmoving mountain flesh. All day
We skied over the endless sleeping shapes;
At dark we men came hungry to our chalet;
All the women were restless at our return,
And they wept while we drank and they cursed us,
Yet we would not rent sleighs pulled by plumed horses
To draw us down the mountain to the Palace
Hotel for champagne, dancing and roulette.
Will women never, never be content?
We let the women weep, looked out at snow,
Thought that all there is to know is snow.

III

They burnt the snowman every spring.
With torches horsemen galloped in a ring,
And at the snowman threw their brands
In time to music from the bands.
Now the guildsmen march away
In ancient, formal guild array;
Yet beyond the Lake of Zurich rise
Stony mountain heads with frozen eyes.

My landlady did not tell me why the bed
Shook so when I awoke shaking at night.
Then I found that trains ran under our house
Back and forth from Paris to Baghdad,
And stopped at Enge Station down the street,
Where passengers stepped out into the snow,
Stretched, then rode on through the tunnel,
Under my bed, into the heart of the beast.
Through the Arlberg, toward the East.

1956

In Tibet in blizzards, priests cut out paper horses
and drop them down the mountainside, whereupon,
it is said, they become live horses for the aid of
persons lost in the storm.

Tonight the world's roof burns,
The yellow roof of the last palace of a living God
Blackens in my dreams: my spirit shrinks in bed.

How childish habits persist! In bed before sleep
I unfold my mind's map in the dark and mark
A place to sleep, a tent near Lhasa,
Where in the distance I see the gold-roofed Potala.
Within the God-King, a boy,
Sleeps in one of its one thousand rooms,
Or wakeful, watches his subjects through a telescope.

In bed before sleep I journey to Tibet to sleep.
In mountain climbing gear, I rise through snow,
Lean into the winds of invisible Everest,
Rest on a gorge's frozen lip, dream there
Of the Abominable Snowman on whose lip, perhaps, I lie;
Then slide, now in real sleep, down a glacier
On the mountain's other side,
As a child on my sled I coasted in Passaic
At night down Aycrigg Avenue, and at the bottom,
By a bonfire, my father stood to take me home to bed
And dreams of coasting down a steeper hill.

Tonight the world's roof burns.
God, a youth in glasses, flees on horseback;
Among sword swinging Khambas circles north,
And at the sound of shots, or demons, stops.
His fur-capped lords then serve him buttered tea.
They wait, twist turquoise earrings, huddle against mules.

But now the oracle speaks, his astrologers concur.
They turn south, wade over drifting snow, scale
The kingdom's ice-faced walls and down;
God descends from his heaven of snow and stone,
From his last kingdom, his last palace,
Where on the roof, still burning, his bodies,
Salted, boiled in butter, face with gilded eyes,
The snow and smoke packed wind. Nearby,
A priest snips paper horses for lost travelers,
Last travelers, loosens them in the wind,
Turning prayer wheels,
Turning oak leaves outside my bedroom window,
Turning clothes on the line my wife has forgotten.

The Inauguration and Shortly After

You could not stop the snow the sky dumped down,
The cold, the lectern smoking when the priest
Invoked the Lord. Did the Lord in answer jab
Your poet blind? Was that your high silk hat
They held against the sun for Robert Frost?
And still he could not see his words for you.
Coatless, then, as if winter were not here
You blow cold words, your hand chops air.

Your wife's French chef breaks skulls
Of eggs. Upstairs her dresser
Gardens in her hair.
A maid brings scented pearls,
The world of Louis and Molière,
Her conquest of Versailles
And Athens. Downstairs
You praise the Spartans.

At the Funeral

Let all those who would stop a war
Sit in a chair and rock
And stare at a woman with flowered hair;
Have her chef prepare
A banquet for all the heads of state:
Let them advance between the Spartan guards,
And past the priest and past the poet.
Let the music play, have them dance,
And rocking in your rocking chair,
Point to a state of possibility:

The fragile arts of peace
Shatter the weather of war.

Now six grey horses draw you to where you are,
Not to Versailles, Sparta, or Athens.
The seventh horse is wild and black
And riderless and paws the streets of Washington
Where you are rocking and will always rock.

John Fitzgerald Kennedy,
You could not stop the shells,
The drowning of your boat in war;
You could not stop the snow the sky dumped down,
The cold, the lectern smoking when your priest invoked
The Lord, your poet struck blind, the bullets in your head,
The six grey horses drawing you to where you are
Rocking and will always rock.

The seventh horse is riderless, wild and black.

Abandoned in the black unmapped unknown
Sierra Nevadas, my tent poles bend
With snow, so hungry I could eat my dog.
Instead of gold I dream of Indian
Stew. Nevada, pup, I wouldn't eat you.
You're too small. You'd make only one poor lunch.
The deer, the immigrants disappeared with snow,
All down the mountain. I am here alone
With wolves, ravens, grizzly bears. I am sick.
I live on venison-bone stew, with luck
A rare raven potpie. Under the snow
If I can find it, if I have the strength
To walk is a dead ox that I can eat.
My head aches, I have fever, hemorrhoids, sores
Open all over my body. The smoke
From my small fire chokes me, blinds me,
Yet in Washington platters heavy with food,
Logs blazing on the hearth, my children there,
I was dying of content. It was in
Dreams that I lived: The King of California,
Gold gushing molten from my mines' mouths; wagons
And ships heavy with ingots. How to live?
It was as if the wind tumbled me westward.
A tornado. I told lies to my wife.
"We will be rich," I said. And all along
I saw the flash of round plump gartered thighs,
Or black eyes of Indian girls I'd have.
Or sitting around the fire broiling buffalo
I'd shot, singing under the stars. All dreams!
We just took off like robins in the fall.
I thought I drove when I was driven west.
Ask me why I am here, I cannot tell.

I dine alone tonight on candle ends
So hungry I could eat up my best friends:
They died of cholera, scurvy, arrows.
And when wagons mired or their oxen died,
They burned the grain, broke their picks and shovels
So no one else could use them, poisoned wells.
They robbed, shot friends, dug up fresh graves for loot.
What would I do now? What *wouldn't* I do now.
I am J. Goldsborough Bruff, President
Of Washington City Mining Company
In my winter palace. Addressing my dog.

Too sick to travel more, left here to guard
Our gear. My men and passing immigrants
All promised to return for me, bring me food.
I'm just 32 miles from Sacramento,
But now the deep snow drifts bury the trails,

And bury what they were and what I was
Or thought I was, and buried my dream of gold,
The triumphal march to the lake of gold
Led by our glorious President Bruff.
How the men hated me. How I hated the men,
Falling asleep with whisky during their watches.
And steal? They even stole my horse. And rape?
Indian women are ugly, such filth:
They are all a starving contemptible race.

Betrayed, Nevada, pup. Who are my enemies?
How can I curse the snow, the cold, the stars?
I have fallen lower than an Indian.
Could I have willed this end, frozen bones buried
In snow, my flesh down wolves' mouths? Map maker

How have I mapped my destiny? I have blamed
My men, I have blamed the snow, my own body,
These legs that won't walk. To be right in all,
And to fall to this. I have led my men
To doors of paradise. I am in Hell,
Alone where white and black are just the same:
Black sky, white snow frozen in darkness, me.

It's getting light Nevada, up and out
Before the sunlight on the snow is blinding.
Up, if I can get up. Out, if I can . . .
I can. I walk like a man on stilts in snow
My snowshoes are heavy as wagon wheels.
God give us game, give us firewood. Each way
I look trackless bare white snow, bare black trees.
I press a long pole through the snow again
And again week after week, a lifetime.
The light blinds me. I am one ache from head
To toe, one running sore. My pole has struck . . .
What? Dig. Dig. I dig with my hands. I feel.
Do I feel the rough frozen hide of ox?
I scrape and shield my eyes from burning snow.
I press my knife with all my weight and cut
Into the golden flesh of ox. I will
Return to Washington, rich, well, honored,
J. Goldsborough Bruff, mapper of the unmapped
West. The gold dust will fall like snow, my pup.

THE LAST WILD INDIAN

For 4,000 years the Yani Indians, numbering about 300, lived
an undisturbed and unchanging life in a territory 40 miles long
and 60 miles wide in the hills of northern California. In 1908
the White men by slaughter had reduced the Yani to one man.
This poem was inspired by Theodora Kroeber's book, *Ishi in
Two Worlds.*

In Golden Gate Park I watch buffalo
Or lie on my back staring with one eye
In my kaleidoscope, buy from a vendor
A penny whistle, then ride the streetcar
To what I call my home, my land, the museum
Where I am its chief exhibit, where I
Am an assistant janitor among crates
Of bones, among the debris of Egypt
And Peru, Greece and Rome. This is my home
On Parnassus Heights where on each Sunday
Afternoon crowds watch me shape arrow heads,
Arrows and bow, the last man of my tribe.

My body that has known no woman's body,
That lived for fifty years among the deer
And rabbits and otter, in winter clothed
With their skins, in summer bare, my body
Feels heavy in shoes, coats, the air heavy
With dead, the rooms with dead men's belongings.
We burn our dead. We keep no keepsakes, nothing.
Our land is perpetually clear, was clear
Until I saw as a child the White Man's
Demon that Mother said was the evil
That followed all White Men, the smoke and clank.
I burned my Mother's body when she died,
And lived three years alone until alone
Was worse than any evil. I gave up

To you who murdered my entire nation,
Who pamper me in this hall of the dead.
They called the Sheriff to the slaughter house,
Then jail, then the long ride in your demon
To the anthropological museum.
When you came in numbers we had not seen
We could not believe earth held so many men,
So many horses, cattle, mules and sheep
And guns to shoot us. We climbed far, high up
In hills away from you. And still you followed.
You did not kill us to eat as cattle,
You killed us to kill us. A noisy kill.
White men smell bad. Before we hunt to eat
We fast and bathe, our breaths clean as air was
In the stony hills, bodies pure of women.

Down wind, I whimper like a fawn or squeak
Like squirrels. Or with fingers on my lips
I make the soft kissing noise of rabbits,
The noise they make when frightened. The arrow
Is silent: The shaft's hazelwood, the feather's
Eagle: my bow covered with a lion's tail,
My quiver skin of one entire otter.
Behind a rock I whimper like a fawn,
I crouch. I listen and hear deer, and wait.
I smell deer. I whimper, and antlers show.
I whimper to draw the great buck up close.
In his eyes I see my eyes shine, and shoot.

My hands are four thousand years old, my hands
Can drill fire from wood, can twirl the man piece
In the woman piece until the sparks glow,
Can chip the heads of arrows from obsidian,
Can shape from mountain juniper a bow
Of such perfection that when I place bow
To my lips and tap the string it will sing

A melody. So more than anything
I love my bow strung with the finest thread
From long tendons of deer I chew and spin.
From boiled skin of salmon we cook our glue.
We waste nothing of what we kill. In fall
With squirrels we gather acorns for mush
To eat in winter in the warm huts where
Women shape baskets, talking their own tongue.
With us all must be clear: Your best drink: tea.
When the hot stones boil the venison stew
It is done: the meat firm and the broth clear.

In my bed in the museum I keep dreaming
Of winter in the hut for men. The sound
Of flint flakers, the tales of grizzly bear,
Or stories of Wood Duck Man, the great hunter
To whom women came: Waterdog Woman,
Waterbug Woman, Bat Woman, Fishhook
Woman, the eyeless Fox Woman, Mountain
Quail Woman, Brown Bear Woman with sweet roots
And herbs. Wood Duck would fling each out his hut
At dawn. Only Morning Star Woman stayed
Past one night, yet she could not catch the heart
Of that hunter whose arrows . . . I am dreaming,
I who have had no woman, will have no
Woman, no children . . . At times of evil,
At moon periods, at times of evil blood,
The women lived alone in separate huts.
With sticks for digging the women would find
Sword fern, redbud, maidenhair, and all stems
And grasses for weaving baskets to hold
The nuts: hazel, pine, buckeye—wild raspberries,
Huckleberries, plums and grapes the children
Would help to pick. The ducks and geese above,
We swam with flying salmon in their streams.
Our lives, rich, plain, turning as the seasons

Turned, at night under our open thatched roofs
We learned stories of stars, the Gods, our Gods.

Here in the museum in San Francisco,
In my new world, holding other old worlds
On Parnassus Heights, I look out the door
At the babble of people, trolley cars,
Autos, the roar of trains, a single plane
Above. I walk to the grocery store
In fog, in smoke, the street vendors clutch me,
So many people, so much noise. Should I
Return to my green hills, the soundless land:
Only bird cries, bees, wind, roar of a bear,
The music of water in which I swim?
In one pocket I have a penny whistle,
In another pocket a kaleidoscope.
Alone in the old world, alone in the new.
Dead in the woods my body would rot unclean,
My soul unclean. Here they promise to burn at death
My body, unlock my soul to shoot back
To heavenly fields of my tribe, my life.
I see through glass of the showcase I polish
The model huts, harpoons, baskets, arrows,
The feather robes. It is snowing. I join
Our father in a hunt for grizzly bear.
My name is Ishi, and Ishi means man.

OFF TO AMAZONIA

I

In middle age
Take the car from the garage
In the garage with hammer and saw
With needle and thread
Build a boat, stitch the sails,
Stow corned beef, water, and rum
Sell the house before it's too late
Say "Good-by. Good-by."
We're off to Amazonia
The last vast emptiness on earth.

Whether to the moon
Or Amazonia
We sail into the past
The lizard watches the jet.
Listen to the wind,
Take a fix from the stars:
Memory.

When I sit I am caving in upon myself,
Broken windows, broken steps, peach pits.

Collect the children
Buy the charts
And mark a route to Belem.

II

Will it be the same?
The roads billowing in red dust,
The armies of immigrants
Yellow eyed with dreams of gold,
Suffocating in the green sea of trees,
All ways pungent with dead animals and men,
Gun fire saluting a new civilization.

Through green rain forests
To grass plains and high table lands
With anteaters, deer, emus
Out of sight of the river
Out of sight of the small Indian tribes
To the land without borders
That is neither Brazil, nor Bolivia, nor Peru
To the land oldest in emptiness
Where our faces in the water
Are the first faces the water has known
To the land fullest of all but men
The newest land.

The wind drives us over the black water
The sun at noon is larger than earth.

Distance seeds the land of fantasy:
It takes imagination to live at home.
Which is more daring: To stay? To go?
The white foam in the wake
The black waters at the prow.

III

In Amazonia we pick the ripe berries,
We rise at dawn, sleep when the sun falls
Swim naked . . .

Through the underbrush they come hacking,
The deer vanish to the sounds of axe and shovel.
At night cards shuffle
The breeze sweats tobacco and gin,
Blows to us the coughs of the dying.

Our boat is becalmed off Florida
The lights of Miami extinguish the moon.
Why do we want to be alone?
How long can we bear to be alone
On the sea, down the river, through the jungle?
What is hidden in the jungle?
Why do we hide in the jungle?

The divan on which I stretch is piled with pillows,
Indigo, silver, plum.
The children swim in the tepid waters of the bay.
I must rise to buy more gin and tonic
3 limes, 2 pounds of scallops
At night in the yacht club from my barstool
I hear the slap of baywater
The bar voices slosh in my ears,
My mind is at sea.

IV

We are not going to Amazonia
This year or next
The car still lives in the garage,
The boat, blueprints in an envelope
We are not going to Kenya or Tibet.
I test the bay water with my toe.

Lashed to my comforts,
I cling to the ordinary,
A mussel on a rock,
Hightide underwater, low above,
Nights. Days. Nights. Days.
The moon is as enchanting as ever
Life is enchanting.

I lurch down the street on my sea legs
Casting invisible winks to invisible girls
I am off to Amazonia.
Faster. Faster. The years—white foam in my wake.

1 *A Mother to Her Young Daughter*

My dream, as all dreams do, came true,
Yet the dreaming was not at all the same:
Certainly the Prince on his charger came,
But the hoof beats tearing earth were louder
And his eyes larger and wilder
When he took me than in my lifelong dream.
He rode away without saying a word,
Leaving servants to take me home—his home.

When the minstrel sang at night to his lute,
(My nipples cracking under my son's hard gums)
The old dream came back, a pale, thin thing,
An uprooted weed that withered while he played
In the cold hall, the Prince always gone.
I took the gentle minstrel for my lover,
Soon hated him, so ordered him slain,
And rubbed his blood on my milk-heavy breasts.

My Prince returned rich with captive women,
His eyes hot with fever, conquest and drink.
When I brought him his son, he did not know me.
When he did not come to me, I slew his women
And sent him their eyes on a small gold tray.
That night with laughter he called me his Queen.
And now my daughter let me hearten you:
Though the dreaming is not at all the same,
Your dream, as all dreams, as mine, will come true.

I was born to fireworks and a drum.
My father lashed the darkness from our palace
To the shore, and burned the sea in oil.
My father kept the drum beat at my crib,
Forbade my mother to rock me in her arms.
My father said that I must be my father's son.

When I could walk he gave me a friend to hit,
And sent up rockets the day I broke his skull.
My father beat me, he said, to teach me pain,
And once he tied me naked at night in snow.
The women my mother sent me always screamed.
When I was seventeen he marched on Spain and died.

For five years in a tower I have heard
A drum beat through my bars and in my sleep,
Where men march in metal, eyes locked ahead.
Row after row they pass through marble doors;
They never move aside, they never return.
It is as if they have never been...or always been...

These long rows of men wading from the sea
Toward palaces of bronze and stone,
With torches they burn long roads in the dark.
They come to the urgent stroke of a drum
Pulsing in a tower where I plot escape . . .
I was born to fireworks and a drum.

I sing old songs to statues in the gardens
Of my King, whom I have served with grace.
Even children are weary of playing here
At the clogged fountain where grass grows wild and long
Over heads of children
Where no lovers come to hear my song.

In the abandoned gardens of my King vines wire
Waist to waist these naked lovers cut in stone.
Arms and heads lie separate in grass
That grows wild and long over their standing thighs.
Torn from body,
A head turns upward to hear my song:

Her marble cheeks still swollen, lids shut, lips
Half-parted in love's last accord, a breath held
Still unbroken in the gardens of my King,
Where my music drew our Queen to her lover
Behind the fountain
Where my dead King dismembered them so long ago.

Up here with apparatus, books,
I sift the stars and never sleep.
Below my butcher king grinds meat,
Will grind the world to smack his taste.
I never whipped an appetite for flesh;
When I was small my blood hung sour,
And spirits mother promised never came.
Stars have beauty only to a fool.

Inside a book I clamp the stars,
The king his subjects on a wheel.
To the worn lips of my eye,
I apply my apparatus,
Inch out the shell; extended, swing,
Probe in the heavens for something,
A sign of . . . I don't know what. Retract.
Here is my horoscope tonight:

From a turning stone, sparks will fly;
The stars are grinding up the sky;
Milk will sour, meat mold, plague follow;
What is today will be tomorrow.
My mother told me in my sick bed
The stone she prayed to and the stars
Were gentle—and my mother's dead.
Stars have beauty only to a fool.

v *The Sisters*

Sisters who go to dark palaces to weep
Before wood, or stone, or screen
Where light of stars whirled through glass—crowned heads—
Flickers on the scene,

The dome above you whirs with wings of gods
And angels caught who watch the death below
Unreel all day and night before their eyes.

Sisters who go to cook, to wash and clean
On hardened knees, who sit in black with beads,
Crossing your lives with these projected deeds,

Can you now before this palace altar,
For these shifting silk embroidered stoles,
Exchange your rags and mops and sinks?
Or bent in rows only weep at your places
Beneath the set immortals' dimming faces?

IX

Some custom stronger than church-going wheels us each summer
From city to shore where we strip habits of the year,
Declare bodies for sun, tides to wash.
We arrive not knowing why we came, except for change;
As last year, years before, an uncle less, a child more—the same.

I

I squat on skeletons spat from the sea;
Stare at water, water's dead.
Near mounds of jellyfish, my flesh
Bears all the puffy age I dread,
Yet an asteroid in my hand retains its points
And clams can stuff their flesh inside their bones,
Then lock their joints.
Tough luck I am a man
So gone to flesh. I do what I can:
Provide my young shovels and a kite;
Let them dig to China, that old world,
Or string a new one in the sky. My son
Wades in to engineer the next world in sand,
Then buries me up to my chin
And rides, a conqueror, on my head.
All life squats on powdery skulls of the dead.

II

My body underground, I search for the horizon,
And see only a blur of fog that screens the edge;
Yet who can mark where beach or sea begins?
Death and life meet in this gray smear,
Shift, cross, for a moment, as lovers, are the same.

My eyes close: a wrong turn
Off the highway, a dark dead end.
My motor fails, mind goes flat.
I wait for the giant wrecker to come,
Find and tow me home.

I wait listening: a shell,
I hold myself to my ear,
Yet I hear nothing
But motors of the sea,
Wheels quarreling
Before wheels of man.

At last my ears attune,
All quarrels turn to song,
And string sounds rise, pour in waves:
Sounds fill me until only sound exists—
Sound sun and stars once made,
And light recorded on our sea
Is now replayed from water's memory,
Record of our seed in sound,
Around, around,
World lost, world found.

Do dead stars fallen from their tracks,
Extinguished notes, heaped shells
On dead ends of the universe
Fill with water's sound, the past, their past within,
Fill until they are nothing yet everything,
Audible motion that will never still?

God grows in my ear's shell;
His toenail pokes my skull.

But Watson,
Holding a starfish in your hand,
You are no star and never were.
You are no one in particular.
What son, indeed? What seed?
Your name will never tell.
You are everything and an empty shell.
What son begat Watson begat Watson?
A seed, a pod, a sound,
And one by one they drowned.
Dogs and sonar towers on the beach
Hear sounds your ears will never reach.

O Watson is dead, but he will rise
Wearing starfish instead of eyes.

III

A detonation in the world above, a flame.
Has the last excavation begun?
Does the wrecker finally come
With chain and hoist?
Gentle music, water in my ear,
The universe leaks out.

It is the young, lolling on treacherous sand
With portable radios to moor them to land.
From their center a girl springs elastic flesh
Between me and the Atlantic
Which she smothers.
She watches shore to see who watches her.
This girl's flesh resurrects me from my grave.
I overthrow my son; he tumbles from my head.
Shall I cartwheel across the sand and dive?

Stop! Back to your grave old man
So run to flesh.
You held the universe like change
In pockets of your ears.
Spend all that for her? Too late. Too late.
In male form, young and beautiful as she,
A lifeguard come to rescue,
Jumps between her and me.

In looking from their flesh to ours,
I see we have a kind of beauty too:
Ignore a line off plumb, a blur,
My wife and I are as beautiful as they.
The swimming mackerel cannot tell,
I'm sure, one human swimmer from another.

A camera clicks; my body is immortal;
My jellied flesh flies to the lens.
Flattened and dried, transformed to celluloid,
It will project over screens in future years
The same: Between children and wife
Back to land, squinting out to sea,
A man stands stripped to his loins.

IV
The sea rolls in white-sheeted sleep;
Motions my flesh to its cold bed,
In which I sink, shivering,
Open-eyed, a figure in a dream,
The sea's dream of itself.
Deep in its mind
I swim toward darkness,

A sunken island
That at night when I swim in sleep
Seems at bottom of sleep,
Yet awake I cannot recall
Ever docking at that island
Which may, as memory
Be a mirror on the floor
Where waver from above the sea
What grains of light
Wheel spinning through topless space
And wheeling each grain is
A broiling contention that is a star,
Wild in self war as war on space.

Projected on a screen
I saw once what was no dream:
Wind rip water,
Water a burning ship
Shelled by a submarine;
A sailor wheel, stab his mate,
And jump to the one last lifeboat seat.

Wind, water, fire accelerate
What gas of space began,
And man must imitate
A glass that lightning makes of sand.

Fish swoop
At hull,
At porthole glass,
At eyes behind a beating fist now still,

At burning eyes,
Green mirrors of stars,
Sodden flames that hum
What we know at heart, the heart.
Black Angels unseen in night now pass
His bubbles of eyes burnt down to gas.

Bless eyes of Robert Wright,
Fog on some ocean island's floor.
Bless Charles Stretch, bless Hartmut Arntz,
Who died from war.
Bless my parents, grandparents
Watson, Trimble, Swett, Berdan,
Back to where we all began;
And back again:
My wife, my son, my daughter,
Their progeny and me.
Bless solids, liquids, gas,
Whatever comes, to pass.

My thoughts plunge below,
Swarm in rows around the sunken hull
Swept under the sea's rug, under its bed.
Ears popping, all air consumed I waken,
Rise awkward as a submarine,
Above my own, the ocean's dream.
Too deep for me this foreign element.

V
I ride breakers,
Wade out again,
Swing through creation,

All past, the sun,
Wheel back and out
And back again
Until all motion,
Time,
I am its pendulum.

The sea coughs,
Spits in space;
I splatter beachward
On my face.

Rest, rider, rest.
Bring fried clams and beer,
Ointments, tape, towels.
Bring sleep, bring girls.
And under an umbrella a woman
Changes; from her bodice drops
A fallen heaven of pearls,
Pearls of my catechism: sleep.
Immortal flesh picked clean,
Immortal mind drained,
Awash I sleep in sun.

VI
The bladder of fog over our horizon,
Inflates as a dirigible, swells
Over beach, over us.
Sun, water, sand, lifeguard, girl
Of elastic flesh—all flesh,
Drawn as dust in a vacuum cleaner,
Become gray gas within its sides,

Ghosts in dust of vacant house,
Shuttered, chairs in shrouds.
All voices, voices on a telephone,
Unanswered, a buzzing sound and gone.
Our family, hand in hand, drifts
Over invisible earth toward light,
Where we specters turn to flesh
In our bath house on the parking lot.

Air that pumped the fog so huge
Between the sun and sand,
Now sucks all fog away.

VII

Under blankets on dunes we watch the townsmen
Wheel new worlds of fire against the night's,
Pump rockets in its side, explode all dark.
They light a bonfire with ten tons of sticks,
A thousand rubber tires, on top a boat.
Tonight they scorch the sky that scorches us.
A marching band with drum sticks flays in time
The ashen skin of air.
While children dance in orbits on the sand,
Above the wind that blew the fog away
Blows out our stars: A puff, a hiss, they drown.
Our flag of liquid fire drops, self-devoured, down.

The boat sinks to its crematorium;
Cars with sleeping children wheel toward home,
Where we shall bed, boarded and bricked
From all elements but one,
That all I father, O father, and the sea fathers
Are: Fog flows past our screen, the glass,
Brings, through our window frame, a burning boat.

Independence Day, Nauset Beach

LIGHT VERSE

A DREAM OF A DREAM OF NIGHT

Night won't leave me alone when I worn down
By Day who whips me through his hoops, his watch
In hand, when I undress for bed to read
In peace alone, Night pesters the door knob,
Stuffs sweet scented pollen under the sill,
And rubs her lips on my window whispering,

"Come out. Come out. I'm raring to go."
"No. It's too late. I'm tired. No. No."
"Please come out. We'll make love under my stars."
"Leave me alone. I've got a wife and child."
"You coward, they can't see you in my dark."

There was no right answer I could make to Night
Except to leave the front door light burning.
I locked doors and windows tight, drew shades,
Too tired for yielding or not yielding.

It was late when I thought Night had gone.
When I fell in bed it was nearly dawn,
But under the bed clothes I felt a form,
Hair that was not Margery's on my cheek,
Stiff black hair across my mouth. *"It's me. Come on,"*
Said Night, *"I love you with all my soul."*
And fell upon me like ten tons of coal.

                            each morning
To stick the live, the dead oak up
Outside my window when my eyes
Come unstuck, before my feet hit
The floor to unroll the lawn—brown—
Unpack the fence, the house next door,
Let down one of their skies (Today's
Is soot grey), spray in temperature,
Hand out noises to the children,
Give me a beard before I get
To the mirror over the sink.
And the way they bring the air back!
It beats me. All night they subtract,
Pulling mean tricks, like sending you
To work without your pants, shooting
At you, even burning down the house.
Once they struck me with a lightning bolt
On the stairs. I knew I was dead.
I did a circus front flip landing
On my head, but it didn't hurt.
I was pleasantly dead a second,
Then they rushed back the windows
With the live, the dead oak glued on
And I unstuck my eyes again
And made darn sure I got my pants
Put on, belt and buckle put on right.

SUN RIME

The piano is out of tune
My bicycle has a flat
Now that our clothes are stolen

We sun ourselves on a dune.
Next week I will look for work
But today is a semi-colon

Between the measles and the mumps
When we idle in sight of the sea
And the sunlight polishes our rumps

The picnic basket is empty
So we begin to kiss
You fell asleep, and so did I.

I CAN'T GO AWAY

Matter, they say, just won't go away,
Though it can change to energy, dirt or smoke.
I won't go away.
The dead won't go away.
See the photographs in our album fade,
Aunts, uncles fading,
Yet forever spooning words in my mouth
That I must say,
Drawing my picture in mirrors.
Will nothing ever, ever go away.

Those stubborn dead impossible to kick back
Or smack.
We pulled down Grandma's house
Cemented her lawn
But she still bosses Mother,
You can't tell me she's gone.

Court the dead and they suck you dry.
The lady up the street gone grey skinny
In her husband's twenty year shut up house
Keeps his shirts starched up ready.
Ready for what I'd like to know?
I'd rather be almost anything than dead.
I'd even rather be alive than dead.
Maybe though when my time comes
They'll have thought up a stunt, new bombs
To make matter permanently go away.

ADVERTISEMENT PAID FOR BY MAFIA, INC., DIVISION OF PHYSICAL PLEASURES

Tell me your heart's desire,
For I can provide at a price
The world's largest assortment of vice.
Broker to judges, bishops, kings,
I stock all that a man might require.
Tell me your deepest need;
My grandfather served Wilde and Gide.
What the heart wants is right.
We deliver any hour, day or night.
Have no feelings of shame,
The world is always the same.
See the pictures in my sample album,
Bound in antique vellum,
Of women in every position,
Examined weekly by a Park Avenue physician.
John Stuart Mill, I remember,
Expounded a theory of pleasure;
What is progress, wealth, leisure for
If not the culmination in privacy behind a door
Of every wish, every dream?
(Yes, next Friday she'll be seventeen;
Her complexion is peaches and cream.)
Our tensions demand release.
(My nephew is chief of police.)
I have agents from Iceland to Macao,
Now let me show you another photo:
Here I am with Juan Peron,
There kneeling at Farouk's throne.

But if you have no tooth for the erotic,
Perhaps you would care for a narcotic.
We have researched a splendid cocaine.
(My assistant will puncture your vein.)
Tell me your heart's desire,
And take this advice,
From your old doctor of vice:
Let nature be your guide,
Impulse be your bride,
For when we are old we measure
The wealth of our lives
By recollections of pleasure.
(We also cater to wives.)

Lions roar on Sunday morning early.
The house shakes,
They leap over my bed,
Where I the great hunter curl on pillows
After my safari,
Where harem girls rub my brow,
But lions are lashing me now
With their tails.
The girls run through the tent flaps,
The wine jug breaks,
The silk billows and the tent stakes collapse.
My head is in a lion's mouth,
It is wet, he spits me out.

The lions are in the kitchen burning toast.
The bells of the harem girls ring in the steeples.
The lions have clawed away my bed clothes,
My skin is all goose pimples.
The lions prowl the driveway on bicycles,
I am wide awake in a bed full of icicles.
I know. It is Sunday, it is Sunday morning early.
I rub my fur, claw to the bathroom, and roar,
"For God's sake, it's too early."

His lips told me my neighbor's, our friend's sins.
I locked my ears. "What did the lips say?"
The wordless wiggle said, "I think my friend
Has sinned as I." The eyes above the lips,
Those eyes said, "My friend, friend,
It's you I mean. You must be guilty too."

I do not say I am not like you. I am.
My misery is that I am. I too am tempted to tell
On my neighbor. I confess my sin.
I tell on my neighbor. I have told on you.

The Dutch Elm disease! I wish some chain saw
Would cut me down before what I've got
People catch.
But on a few foolish days each year
When I imagine I am well, I take a nap.
Do nothing! Until GUILT that bad housewife
Begins to scold.
                    "But I'm too sick," I whine.
I slam the door, limp back to the office,
Work late, coveting my neighbor's wife
(Porch-sitting in a wicker chair):
A "bon voyage" fruit basket to take to . . .
Damn it, where?
I was seasick in the Navy and fruit
Is more than ulcers,
Oh more than man can bear.

Back. Back. Look out. Here comes the maniac,
A stout man in black driving a grey Pontiac,

Stolen, who strangled fifteen prostitutes,
And shot three cops and now plucking the fruits

Of evil, his car skids on ice, somersaults
Into the canyon. The end. They play a waltz

To route us up the aisles, out the movie house,
I think of the soft flesh under her blouse.

When I start my grey Pontiac around
The pretzel roads of Topanga Canyon,

I wonder will she or will she not?
Back at her apartment, the door slams shut

In my face, I embrace an empty hall,
O love unrequited I'd need a waterfall

To douse my burning heart. Watch out. Back.
Here comes the maniac in his grey Pontiac.

THE GUM JOY CHINESE-AMERICAN RESTAURANT

Its awning says.
I'll go as soon as I lose my last tooth,
(Yawning toward death)
To pleasure these gums
With some dish erotic in old mouths
After the extraction of desires one by one,
But one remains: the high cuisine,
The meeting of East and West,
When and whereas there shall be no light,
And we shall die with rice tickling our gums.
Behold our great gum joy
Embalmed in tiny cups of green tea.
Right now while whisky lashes your remaining teeth,
Run, be joyous with other parts
And save for last
THE GUM JOY CHINESE-AMERICAN RESTAURANT

On the bus, the beach, at dawn, at dusk,
On barstool, at my bowling alley,
To church, to shop, to mop, to sweep,
To scold the children, with husband
In her arms, I dream, she is asleep,
Those metal curlers, those thorns still
Are worn. Tucked in her coffin will
She persist? And at the great gates too?
No bad breath, acne, ancient belt
Of chastity, nor heart-shaped tattoo,
Can ward off as these curlers do
All lechers, lovers, with such ease.
Lady, whom do you expect to please,
At what moment will you release
Those tortured strands of vile hair,
Stand before your neighbors unmetaled and bare?

A native of Passaic, New Jersey, Robert Watson
was educated at Williams College and The
Johns Hopkins University, and later taught at
both institutions. He attended the University of
Zurich as a Swiss-American exchange fellow,
and is currently Professor of English at the
University of North Carolina at Greensboro. He
is the author of three earlier books of poems,
A Paper Horse, *Advantages of Dark*, *Christmas In
Las Vegas*, and a novel, *Three Sides of the Mirror*.